LIVING
Love

LIVING Love

DEBBIE ALSDORF

Cook Communications

Faithful Woman is an imprint of
Cook Communications Ministries, Colorado Springs, Colorado 80918
Cook Communications, Paris, Ontario
Kingsway Communications, Eastbourne, England

LIVING LOVE

Printed in the United States of America

1 2 3 4 5 6 7 8 9 10 Printing/Year 04 03 02 01 00

Editor: Afton Rorvik
Cover Design: David Thomason
Interior Design: Lisa A. Barnes

Library of Congress Cataloging-in-Publication Data

Alsdorf, Debbie.
    Living love / Debbie Alsdorf.
        p. cm.
    ISBN 0-7814-3383-5
        1. Love—Biblical teaching. 2. Interpersonal relations—Biblical teaching. 3.
    Christian women—Religious life. 4. Bible—Study and teaching. I. Title.

BS680.L64 A47 2000
241'.4—dc21   00-027251

Dedicated to
my sons Justin and Cameron Brier
It is because of my love for you that I made the choice
to learn what it really means to live in God's love.
Though I am still learning, it is my prayer that what has
been planted in your hearts will make a difference in
your relationship with God and with others.

"These commandments that I give you today
are to be upon your hearts.
Impress them on your children" (Deuteronomy 6:6-7).

"So the next generation would know them,
even the children yet to be born,
and they in turn would tell their children" (Psalm 78:6).

"My command is this: Love each other as I have loved you."
John 15:12

ACKNOWLEDGMENTS

It is in the context of relationships that we learn how to walk in God's love. I would like to thank the following people for their influence in my life.

Ray . . . my husband and my friend. You are a true example of putting others first. May we spend our days learning what it means to live in God's love. You are a gift, and I love you (Romans 8:28).

Sharon Montagna . . . my sister, and only sibling. I am thankful we have each other. Through pain we have learned what it means to be "sisters of the heart." Thanks for the "roof" during a most difficult season of life.

Jinny, MaryLou, and Becky . . . my mentors in the walk of God's love and grace. As you lived in God's love before me, I was changed. I will never forget you.

Pauline Davis . . . a precious neighbor. You taught me how to reach out with God's love. The boys and I will never forget how you loved us in practical ways.

Liz Grundvig . . . my friend. You have encouraged me, prayed for me, and faithfully loved me. Thanks! Your friendship inspires me to grow in Christ.

Lisa Woodworth . . . my friend all the way from Aviation High School. God brought us together many miles and many years later for a most wonderful friendship. You continually bring me back to the *bottom line:* God's love. Thank you.

Julie Fox . . . my friend who walks the practical side of love. Your cards and your friendship mean so much to me.

Diane Linse . . . my friend who has come in like an angel to organize my life. In the process you have filled my heart. What a treasure you have been to me. Thanks.

Chuck Smith . . . my very first pastor. Your teaching of God's Word laid the foundation for my life.

Pastor Steve and Brenda Madsen and Pastor Mark Calcagno . . . you have all been an example to me of people who seek to live the love of God.

Thank you for your encouragement. It has been healing.

Julie Smith . . . at ChariotVictor Publishing. Thank you for everything.

The women of Cornerstone Fellowship . . . because of you, I am daily learning more about walking the walk of love. Together may we continue to desire God's heart—forgiving, loving, and accepting one another. We are all in process.

CONTENTS

*I*NTRODUCTION

God loves each of us with an extravagant love. His love goes beyond our mistakes and shortcomings. His love goes beyond our personality quirks, bad days, and bad attitudes. God's love is amazing. It is wonderful when we begin to understand God's love for us personally. But, it's not enough to stop there—God desires to fill us with His love, and teach us what it means to love others.

God calls us to love one another, but we often don't take that command seriously. We add conditions to His command, supposing that there is a menu of different options, depending on our present circumstances or the dynamics of our current relationships.

I have often thought that I could learn to live in God's love if I were living alone on a mountaintop or tucked away in a cave. There in the quietness and peace of not having to deal with other people, I could think about God's love and come up with great theory. In this place of seclusion, I could love everybody and everything. There would be nothing to stop me from love . . . no disappointments, no disagreements, and no conflict.

But, we aren't living on a mountaintop or in the seclusion of a cave. We are living in homes with people that rub us the wrong way, say the wrong things, and often take us for granted. We are working in offices with people of different interests, different backgrounds, and different personalities. Add to the mix, all the complex relationships of today—in-laws, out-laws, and ex-laws—and you have a real challenge.

It's easy to love those who like us, but in real life we often live in the battlefield of misunderstandings. When my children were young, I realized that I could never teach them about Jesus and His love, if I lived in bitterness toward others. I realized it made little sense to speak to them of God's love while holding tightly to resentments, grudges, and bitterness. Because all of my relationships weren't perfect, I had a dilemma. Which direction would I set my heart and my life toward?

God gave me the grace and strength to choose life through His Word instead of choosing spiritual, emotional, and relational death by living according to my selfishness.

Each day I am aware that He continually gives me the grace to choose His love over the alternative. God will give you the grace to live in His love too. It is in this place that we become free—no longer bound by expectations of how people should treat us, but in submission to the will of the Father, which is to "love one another" (John 15:17). Jesus told us to remain in His love, so that His joy would be in us, and our joy would be complete (John 15:11).

Daily we have choices. Living in love is a choice. Your choice to follow after the heart and will of God is simply the starting point. At times it is the most difficult choice you will make—a lip-biting, teeth-grinding choice.

The power for change doesn't come by your choice, but by the power of God's Spirit working on your heart. Though your choice is important in pointing you in the right direction, it is the power of God that will change you from the inside out.

This study isn't about being perfect. It is about pointing your heart in the right direction, and allowing the Word of God to be a compass that will direct your life and your relationships. In this study we will be focusing on what the Bible says about our relationships with other people. You will be looking at Scripture to direct you in your everyday relationships. You will meditate on God's Word to find answers to some of your most practical questions such as:

How do I love those who have hurt me?

What about forgiveness?

How do I handle conflict and still honor God in my relationships?

How, as a Christian, do I balance my feelings with my faith?

You can do this study individually, with a friend, or in a group. You should plan to do some of the study each day, thinking about how God's Word and His way relate to your real life today. Always begin by praying for understanding, asking the Holy Spirit to lead you into the truth of God's design for you as His daughter.

If you do this study in a group, I suggest you work through one chapter a week. Each chapter has eleven to seventeen sections. These can easily be divided into a five-day block by doing three sections each day. Set time aside, even if it is just ten to fifteen minutes to do nothing but soak in Scripture. You will need a Bible, a dictionary, and a thesaurus. You might also find it helpful to have a blank journal in which you can write your personal thoughts while working through the book.

Jesus Christ has the wonderful ability to change us from the inside out. He can heal our hearts, heal relationships, and pick us up where we have fallen down. Together let's set our hearts toward God, making the choice to walk the walk, and not just talk the talk. Let's step into freedom as we learn to live and love God's way. It is a more peaceful and happier way to live!

Learning with you,
Debbie Alsdorf

TIPS FOR GROUP MEMBERS

When working through this study in a group, the following suggestions may prove helpful.

- ∞ Have a purpose for your time together. What do you hope to accomplish in twelve weeks?

- ∞ Keep in step with the lesson, giving opportunity for personal sharing on the topic of each lesson and the message of each Scripture passage.

- ∞ Encourage one another to be real and provide a safe place for that.

- ∞ Keep all group conversation and sharing Christ-centered and confidential.

- ∞ Encourage practical application of each week's lesson, holding each other accountable.

- ∞ Pray before you begin, and pray when you end.

TIPS FOR GROUP LEADERS

It is a privilege to lead other women in the direction of loving others with God's love. The choices they make to love will have a ripple effect on everyone they know. The following suggestions may help you lead each woman in your group in her personal journey of living God's love.

∞ Make every effort to stay on track so that you study the Bible rather than just functioning as a social or support group. Though both social interaction and support are important, the main emphasis should first be the personal application and study of God's Word. (As you know, women can get off track!)

∞ Promote fellowship and unity within the group by accepting each woman right where she is today. Have a "No Stones" policy—women agree not to judge or throw stones at another woman who is struggling and seeking understanding within the group.

∞ Nurture each woman in her spiritual gifts, personal holiness, and in her interaction with the Word of God.

∞ Be real so others can be real too.

∞ Be honest as you work through the study so that others can feel safe confessing their faults and find healing as they learn to apply God's Word.

∞ Help women be accountable as they work through relationship issues.

∞ Pray for each woman in your group and take seriously the privilege of leading her in a study of God's Word.

DAILY PRAYER

So far today, God,
I've done all right . . .
I haven't gossiped.
I haven't been grumpy, nasty or selfish.
I'm really glad of that,
but in a few minutes, God,
I'm going to get out of bed,
From now on, I'm probably going to
need a lot of help.[1]

L IVING HIS LOVE . . . THE KEY TO LIFE

Love is one of the few things in life worth pursuing with a godly passion.

K eys are necessary little pieces of metal that are designed to unlock things. Each key has a unique configuration of curves that make up a pattern expressly designed to free up a particular lock.

God's love is like a key that has been expressly designed to unlock our hearts and the hearts of those we love. Many of us are locked up inside. We are hurting, frustrated, and confused. We need the touch of God's love because His love is the key to salvation, fulfillment, and relationship with Him. We were created for relationship with God and for relationship with others. These relationships can be rewarding, or they can be a disastrous set of unmet expectations.

Understanding God's love for us changes the way we look at ourselves and at our lives. God's love also changes how we look at other people. As we understand His love more personally, we see others as people just like us, who need a touch of God's love too. We also come to realize that it is God's will for us to remain in love and to love others.

We must always keep in mind that it is His Love, given by His Spirit that is the key. No amount of love we could muster up in our own strength will unlock the doors to lasting fulfillment in relationship with others. It is God's love that has the power to change our lives and the lives of those we come in contact with. My ability to love others is directly related to the condition of my own heart before God.

1. Read Hosea 2:7-20.

In this passage we see Hosea's love for his unfaithful wife, Gomer. Her unfaithfulness is a picture of Israel's unfaithfulness in her relationship with God. Instead of responding to God in thankfulness and love, the Israelites offered what they had to idols. They went after things and people to find love and fulfillment, instead of being thankful for God and His love.

∞ According to Hosea 2:8 and 2:13, whom did Israel forget?

∞ Maybe you have a habit of forgetting God. Have you ever experienced God drawing you back to Himself as He did here with Israel? (See 2:14.) Describe your experience.

∞ Write out Hosea 2:19-20.

Betroth comes from a Hebrew word that means pledged, or pledged to be married.[1] It is not a word that we use much today, but the significance of being pledged to another person through the covenant of marriage is still significant. We would probably say engaged instead of betrothed, but the meaning remains the same.

∞ What does this Hosea passage say to you personally, when you stop and think of God pledging His life to you, and yours to Him forever?

◎ Think of what it means to be engaged to someone. It is a connection, an interlocking with, a tie-in with someone, a connection of two hearts. Isn't this the kind of connection Jesus wants with us?

> *I will betroth you to Me forever; yes, I will betroth you to Me in righteousness and justice, and in steadfast love, and in mercies. I will even betroth you to Me in stability and in faithfulness, and you shall know—recognize, be acquainted with, appreciate, give heed to and cherish—the Lord (Hosea 2:19–20, AMP).*

◎ Instead of forgetting the Lord and His love, what does this passage say you should do?

◎ Who or what holds the key to your heart today? (Consider things, people, agendas, or your dreams.)

◎ Can you trust in the Lord enough just for today to give Him the set of keys that you have and ask only, "Thy will be done"?

Write out "I will acknowledge the Lord" (Hosea 2:20) on a 3 x 5 card and carry it with you as a bookmark. Or put it on your car dash, on the refrigerator, or your office desk. Let this card serve as a reminder to always acknowledge (recognize, be acquainted with, appreciate, give heed to, cherish) the Lord. God wants us to acknowledge Him, have a relationship with Him, be betrothed to Him, and in Him alone find the deepest source of love. Oh . . . we get so distracted! But God's love is the key—the necessary component—to living a full life.

◎ Do the following definitions of *acknowledge,* that you just read in Hosea, represent your current relationship with God?

- *Recognize*—Do you recognize Almighty God, your Maker and acknowledge Him?
- *Be aquainted with*—Do you know Him?
- *Appreciate*—Do you thank God from whom all blessings flow?
- *Give heed to*—Do you read His Word and take His instruction seriously?
- *Cherish*—Do you hold close to your heart all that He is?

Each day is a precious gift. Each day also holds within it the ability to cause stress, anxiety, troubles, and disappointments. When these things play havoc with us it's easy to see why we become locked up. It's as if we are bound from seeing the things of the Spirit because we are so focused on everything else around us. It is vitally important to have the right key, *Jesus*, that will unlock us from the distress and the loveless times we experience in the "real world."

2. Read Matthew 16:13-19.

In verse 15, Jesus asks who Peter thinks He is. This question is just as appropriate for us today. People hold so many different opinions about Jesus. Nearly all world religions acknowledge Him, but not all religions acknowledge that He is the Messiah or the Son of God. Many don't realize that He is still alive. Christian faith is based on the death and resurrection of Jesus Christ. Christians should believe in a living God. It is because He lives that we can face any relationship, any challenge, any insult.

∞ Is your relationship with God alive? How do you know?

∞ Do you believe in a living God? Why or why not?

∞ What was Jesus' response to Simon Peter's answer? (Matthew 16:17)

∞ According to this passage, who reveals to our hearts the reality of who Jesus Christ is? (If you are still uncertain about who Jesus really is, ask God to show you.)

3. **Read John 17, the entire chapter.**

As you read, keep in mind that this is Jesus praying. Pay close attention to what He is saying to the Father about you.

In John 17, I find hope in the following truths.
- He has authority over me (v.2).
- He gives me eternal life (v.3).
- I am His (v.10).
- I am protected (v.12).
- I am given joy (v.13).
- I have His Word (v.14).

∞ Write out John 17: 15-17.

Sanctify means to set apart. Here Jesus is asking the Father to keep us set apart by the Word of God, which is the truth. He also tells us that the truth of His Word will set us free (John 8:32). We can see that it is the heart of Jesus and the plan of God, that we would be *set apart and set free.*

Unlocked from the patterns of this world, we become free to love God's way. We become free to live in the will of our Father. We become free to have a relationship with God, the maker of all things, including our hearts and the hearts of others.

4. **Write out John 17:26.**

> I made Your name known to them and revealed Your character and Your very Self, and I will continue to make [You] known, that the love which You have bestowed upon Me may be in them—felt in their hearts—and that I [Myself] may be in them (John 17:26, AMP).

∞ What does Jesus pray will be in you?

He Himself in me? Wow . . . now that is a powerful possibility! Even as I write this, I am getting ready for a meeting with a woman who is demanding, difficult, and rude. Her agenda for today is to chew me up! Could it be that God could express His very character to this woman through me today? Could He possibly give me the grace to be kind to someone who is mistreating me?

> *It's a wonderful day indeed when we stop working for God and begin working with God.*
> *– Max Lucado* °

Once we recognize (get it firmly established in our minds) that God Himself lives in us and wants to work through us, life becomes different. It is this type of lifestyle that I liken to an "E" ticket ride. I know that I am dating myself, but the "E" ticket was the best ticket in the park, back in the early days of Disneyland. It was the Matterhorn!

Life can be an "E" ticket as we experience the exciting adventure of watching the power of a living God change us and work in and through us. Or, it can be an "A" ticket—that was the Abraham Lincoln Theater—a slow, just-trying-to-get-by lifestyle. God wants the best for His children, and the best is believing the truth and living in its power each day.

5. **Write out Matthew 16:19.**

Some people use this verse to claim all kinds of things that God never claimed would be unlocked for them. Naming and claiming can leave us confused and disappointed, if what we are naming and claiming is not God's will for us. But, it is safe to say that living in God's love is definitely God's will for us. He gives us the keys of love, the keys of His kingdom, so that His character might be unlocked in us. It is by the love of God that we can become content, joyful women who are filled with hope and security.

It is God's love that will:
set us apart for His purposes
and
set us free to love others.

Everything that pertains to life was given to God's Son, and now He gives it all to us. As Jesus walked on this earth, the love of the Father filled Him. It was no ordinary love that gave Jesus the courage to go to the cross. It was the extraordinary love of the Father that compelled Him to commit His life to the will and plan of God. It is this same love that compels us to give our all to Jesus.

No other love will be sufficient for the tasks that He has planned for us. No other love will withstand insult and injury. No other love will give us the capacity for forgiveness. Nothing but the love of God will enable us to go the extra mile!

Pray that this love of God will be unlocked and poured out on your everyday life. His love let loose on earth through you is an exhilarating experience. Seek God for His love and seek to be a vessel of that love.

A vessel of love is simply a woman God can flow through to love others. As we are filled up with Christ, we can be poured out for others. In this way, we can be God's instruments of love and peace. People moving with the heartbeat of God.

6. Read John 15:4-7.

☙Where must you remain if you are going to bring forth the fruit of God's love?

> "This is the rock on which I will put together my church, a church so expansive with energy that not even the gates of hell will be able to keep it out. And that's not all. You will have complete and free access to God's kingdom, keys to open any and every door: no more barriers between heaven and earth, earth and heaven" (Matthew 16:18–19, TM).

> I will give you the keys of the kingdom of heaven, and whatever you bind—that is, declare to be improper and unlawful—on earth must be already bound in heaven; and whatever you loose on earth—declare lawful—must be what is already loosed in heaven (Matthew 16:19, AMP).

> God wants to be as close to us as a branch is to a vine. One is an extension of the other. It's impossible to tell where one starts and the other ends. The branch isn't connected only at the moment of bearing fruit. The gardener doesn't keep the branches in a box and then, on the day he wants grapes, glue them to the vine. No, the branch constantly draws nutrition from the vine. Separation means certain death.[3]—*Max Lucado*

∞ What are you like, when not living the connected life? (See John 15:6.)

7. Write out the different aspects of the fruit of God's Spirit as found in Galatians 5:22.

∞ Do you think these qualities would be helpful in personal relationships? Explain.

∞ How do you get this fruit?

Remember, fruit is a by-product of the branch being connected to the vine. When the branch gets its nourishment from the vine, fruit grows naturally and freely. In the same way, God's love and the fruit of that love, will naturally become evident in you as you live the connected life. Connected to Christ Himself. This kind of fruit doesn't just happen by our involvement in church, good works, good choices, or willpower. It is produced by a life connected to the Father. A life that is receiving power and love each day from the source of all power and love.

8. **Read John 15:5-12.**

Take note of the following verses and write out how each one can apply to your personal life.

∞ *verse 5:* If a woman remains in Christ and Christ remains in her, she will bear the fruit of love, joy, peace, etc.

∞ *verse 8:* Bearing the fruit of Christ brings the Father glory.

∞ *verse 9:* Remaining in the Father's love is staying connected in relationship with Him and obeying His Word.

∞ *verse 11:* By remaining in the Father's love, our lives and our joy is complete.

9. **Write out John 15:12.**

∞ How has the Father loved you?

∞ What are some of the characteristics of the Father's love toward you? (Galatians 5:22)

10. **Read John 15:13-17.**
∞ How can you become God's friend?

11. Now write out John 15:16-17.

∞ What did God appoint for you to do?

∞ What is His command, and how does this relate to your life and relationships today?

12. Journal your thoughts on the following questions.
  • How do you bear fruit?

  • What kind of fruit are you to produce?

  • What has Jesus clearly commanded you to do?

  • Does your lifestyle need an adjustment to fulfill this command?

The Word of God clearly tells us that God has poured His love into our hearts by the Holy Spirit (Romans 5:5).

We can do nothing of eternal lasting value without being connected to our Heavenly Father. The choice then that counts, is the choice to live connected to the Father—abiding and remaining in Him. This is the key. In desiring to live God's love toward others, it is very important never to lose sight of this foundational truth.

We want to love, but sometimes people are unloving, difficult, obnoxious, or hurtful. There are other times when we really want to love, but we are hurting, needy, or just too tired to be bothered with thinking of everyone else.

This is exactly why we need to rely on a fresh flow of God's love into our hearts and lives each day. It must be His love that flows through us. When it is His love working in us and through us, we can move through life, learning to love despite the others' responses or our own current emotional energy level.

> *Such hope never disappoints or deludes or shames us, for God's love has been poured out in our hearts through the Holy Spirit Who has been given to us (Romans 5:5, AMP).*

13. Write out Romans 5:5 and memorize this verse. It is important to remember the source of love is always Jesus and not yourself or others!

God's love is the key. And, His Spirit is the locksmith, waiting to dispense to you what is needed to open the hearts of the people that God has placed in your life. Your part is going to the Father for His wisdom, His guidance, His strength, and the love of His Spirit. We must pray and ask that the love of God would be evident in our lives, and that His love would actually love others through us—through our touch, our words, our smile, our actions, and so on. The people in our lives better fasten their seat belts because by the power of God's Spirit, love is coming their way!

> *We are never left feeling short-changed. Quite the contrary—we can't round up enough containers to hold everything God generously pours into our lives through the Holy Spirit (Romans 5:5, TM).*

It is my prayer that you will become convinced through the evidence in God's Word that walking in love is exactly the path He intended for you. It will take you a step toward unbroken communion with the Father. As you step closer to this type of relationship, you will begin moving in the ways of the Spirit. Love will be the by-product of your personal interaction with Christ.

∞ Did this lesson help you understand where to begin if you are really going to learn how to love God's way? Explain.

Father,

I ask You to fill me with Your love. Come now and pour through my life and draw others to You through the power of Your love working in and through me. I realize that loving others might be a challenge, but I ask You to do the impossible inside of me. I commit to You those whom You have placed in my life and in my path. Give me Your love for them and show me how to walk in Your way toward those You have put before me. My prayer is that Your love will become the focus of my life. Amen.

LIVING LOVE . . . IN OUR DAILY CHOICES

Love is making another feel valued,
significant, and worthwhile.

Christians don't love automatically. It is a fact that we are ordinary people—human beings with fleshly tendencies. But, many of us think that love should flow out of our every pore once we have committed our lives to Christ. Unfortunately, there is no automatic love switch that is flipped on when we come to Christ. We come to Christ just as the human flesh we are . . . no more, no less. And, as we surrender our lives and our wills to Him, things in our lives begin to take a different shape. It is a process.

Spiritual growth does not happen overnight. In the same way, learning to relate to others God's way is a process of growth and surrender. Loving God's way is the process of recognizing our value to God, and in turn recognizing others' value.

Insecurity is probably the biggest culprit of bad relations between women. When we are insecure, we easily become threatened by others, and find it hard to honestly esteem others with the significance and value they deserve as God's own beloved children. Women in record numbers suffer with insecurities and low self-esteem. Even within churches, women silently suffer with feelings of being less than okay.

When you begin to grasp God's great love for you, and that reality goes from head knowledge to the heartbeat of who you are, you will become convinced that you should honor others with that same wonderful love.

If you are struggling with insecure thoughts and feelings of worthlessness, you need to spend some time soaking in God's love for you. Allowing the truth in God's Word to penetrate those insecurities will be the first step in personal wholeness and stability. I encourage you to memorize verses on God's love. Sit with the message of love. Think about what it says to you individually. In time, your low self-esteem and insecurity will be replaced with peace and confidence. As you fill yourself with God's Word and His thoughts and truth, you will become more equipped for loving others because you will understand the very nature of God's love.

1. **Read Joshua 24:14-24.**
∞ According to this passage, what were the people of Israel committing themselves to do?

∞ What were two things that had to go, if they were to make this choice? (v. 23)
   1.
   2.

2. **Read Deuteronomy 30:19-20.**
∞ Write out verse 19.

∞ What are you to choose?

∞ What will making this choice accomplish in your life?

Because God did not program us as robots, we have the possibility of choice. Loving others and choosing God's way will not be an easy adventure. It will be a challenge. Perhaps one of the most difficult challenges you have ever faced. You are probably thinking, *Wait a minute! I thought you said God's love was going to pour through me, how could that be a challenge?*

Well, the challenge comes in making the CHOICE to love. You must make a choice to follow God's way rather than submitting to your own self-ish heart. The choice itself does not empower you, God's Spirit does the empowering. Your choice simply sets your heart in a given direction.

In Joshua 24:15, Joshua told the Israelites, "Choose for yourselves this day whom you will serve." Joshua knew that there was a choice to be made—a directional choice. Once we say, "Lord I choose You and Your way of loving others over my ways," God begins to work His love into our deep-est parts. But, it is a journey, a process, and a daily learning experience. There is no quick fix. Each day we have a choice! Choose this *day* whom you will serve. Will it be yourself, or will it be God? If you choose to serve yourself, then surely your love will be conditional at best. If you choose to serve God, then the power of God's Spirit will work in you, enabling you to love in an unconditional Christlike fashion.

The power comes from God, and the power of God is made available to us through relationship with Jesus Christ.

3. Read 1 John 3:11-24 and think about the following questions.

co What is the message that has been preached since the beginning? (v. 11)

co What have you passed from, and why? (vv. 14-15)

co What are you to choose each day? (Deuteronomy 30:19)

co What is the pattern for relationships that Jesus left for you to follow? (1 John 3:16)

co How are you to love? (vv.17-18)

∞ What is God's commandment? (v. 23)

4. Write out Proverbs 8:10.

∞ Read Proverbs 8:32-36.
Can you see the clear distinction between choosing life over death?
Describe it in your own words.

∞ What will make us wise women? (v. 33)

∞ There are three components here to blessing. What are they? (v. 34)
1.
2.
3.

When we are daily listening, watching, and waiting on God, we receive favor and blessing. Blessed are those who keep His ways! (Proverbs 8:32) His way is the path of love. Though it is not always an easy choice, it is the choice that will keep us connected to God and in fellowship with Him.

5. Write out 1 John 4:11-12.

∞ What is made complete in you when you love others?

6. Read Proverbs 16:16, 20.
Here we see the choice factor again. Choose understanding . . . go for

it, line up with it, take hold of it because it is better than anything money can buy! God's ways are different than ours. His ways are higher, His ways are a challenge to our small reasoning. Our reasoning revolves around us, and that is very small. It is important to look for God's instructions for life.

∞ Write out Proverbs 16:25.

∞ Have you ever wanted your own way when in the middle of a relationship issue? Explain.

∞ Describe a time when you felt justified in holding your grudges, score-keeping, or in maintaining your unforgiving attitude.

∞ Do you believe that your way leads to death, and God's higher road of love leads to life? Why or why not?

∞ Which way will you choose? Why?

7. **Read John 7:16-18.**
∞ What does this passage say to you regarding choice and choosing God's way?

8. **Read Philippians 2:1-4.**
∞ Write out Philippians 2:4.

∞ Now make a list of people with whom you are in contact on a regular basis. These are the people that God has placed in your life. Not one of these relationships is an accident. The list might include immediate family, other relatives, coworkers, neighbors, ex-spouse, in-laws, ex-laws, friends, children, etc.

> *For it is God who works in you to will and to act according to His good purpose (Philippians 2:13).*

This is your target list. Your daily choices create a ripple effect—either good or bad—that touches all lives around you. Your goal with this list is to leave the mark of Jesus in your relationships with these people that God has placed in your life.

Some people on this list are easy for you to love. You may have the same interests, personalities, for example. Others are difficult if not downright impossible to love. But God promises to give us all that we need if we choose His way over ours.

Let's look at how the Bible addresses the impossible challenges, such as loving the unlovable.

9. **Write out the following verses that address the word *impossible*.**
   • Luke 1:37

   • Luke 18:27

   • Matthew 17:20

   • Hebrews 11:6

After writing out these Scriptures, do you still think it is impossible to love some of those people on your list? What about when you are worn out, and too tired to even crack a smile? Impossible? What about when someone has hurt you so deeply that you just want to run and hide? Impossible? Your problems are now God's possibilities!

It is not impossible for us to love because we have the source of love living inside of us. But we must remember that it is God's love and not a counterfeit or fake love that we want to pour through us. It is a genuine work of the Spirit that we are trusting God for in our relationships. He is the source.

∞ Journal your thoughts here.

10. Read 1 Corinthians 13. Now let's look at love.

Many people refer to this passage as the Love Chapter of the Bible. We can see in this chapter the characteristics of God's love toward us, and we can also see God's pattern of loving others with that same love. For example: God is patient and kind with us, and it is His patience and kindness that can pour out through us to others as well. These attributes of God's love are the very traits that He can work into our hearts and lives as we abide in Him. His love is our pattern.

∞ Make a list of the qualities of love—the patterns of Christ that you see in these verses.

∞ Do these qualities also characterize you in your relationships with others?

11. Write out 2 Timothy 2:22.

∞ According to this verse, what are the four things you are to pursue?
1.
2.
3.
4.

∞ Look up the dictionary definition of *pursue* and write it here.

I like this definition of *pursue*: to chase or run after. This definition helps me to see clearly that a directional choice is the first step. If I am running after something, I am progressing in a given direction. I have a goal, and I am going toward that goal. Today I want to make a choice to chase after love! I can see clearly that it is God's will to pursue, follow after, chase, and choose love.

Based on 1 John 4:16, we see that God is love. In 1 Corinthians 13, we see the characteristics of God's love. Living a life of love is a change in lifestyle. Living love is different from living in our own natural tendencies and our own behaviors toward people. We naturally love those who love us, but now God has a better way.

12. Read 1 John 4: 7-12.
∞ What is the main theme of this passage?

∞ Where does love come from?

∞ What is made complete in you if you love others? (v. 12)

13. Read 1 John 4:13-16.

∽ Have you acknowledged that Jesus is the Son of God?

∽ Who lives in you at that point of acceptance and acknowledgment? (v. 15)

∽ On what then do you rely?

The focus here is on the fact that God loves us; therefore, we are to love others with the same love that has been freely given and poured into us. We don't deserve the love of God. Many people that you know do not deserve your love either—just thinking about their actions may make you cringe. Yet, just as we are not perfect, God calls us to a higher place of loving other imperfect ones. If we are to continue on in the Lord, we must daily choose to set our hearts toward a LIFESTYLE CHANGE of love.

Living to love should be our life pursuit. This lifestyle of love should be our goal because Jesus himself clearly outlined in the Gospels that it was His plan for us to be a loving people. This pursuit is clearly not based on making ourselves happy, but on making Jesus master of our lives. In so doing we will also become happy women. Why? Because when we put God and His Word first, we are walking in the Spirit. The mind set on the Spirit is full of peace (Romans 8:6). Jesus tells us in John 15:11 to remain in His love, then He lets us know why He has given this instruction: "so that my joy may be in you and that your joy may be complete." Do you want joy? Remain in His love!

The world we live in has purpose and joy all turned around. The focus is on being true to ourselves and pleasing ourselves. But all we get when we live to please ourselves is a selfish, self-absorbed heart. Living to please God and love others will take us out of the empty world of self and into new heights with our heavenly Father. A place where we experience the fullness of joy as His joy is in us and our joy is complete.

Learning to love when it is not convenient is part of this lifestyle change. Just look at the words of Max Lucado as he illustrates this point in the following story.

My first pet came in the form of a childhood Christmas Eve gift. Somewhere I have a snapshot of a brown-and-white Chinese pug, small enough to fit in my father's hand, cute enough to steal my eight-year-old heart. We named her Liz.

I carried her all day. Her floppy ears fascinated me, and her flat nose intrigued me. I even took her to bed. So what if she smelled like a dog? I thought the odor was cute. So what if she whined and whimpered? I thought the noise was cute.

Mom and Dad made it clear in our prenuptial agreement that I was to be Liz's caretaker, and I was happy to oblige. . . . Within a few days, however, my feeling changed a bit. Liz was still my dog, and I was still her friend, but I grew weary with her barking and she seemed hungry an awful lot. More than once my folks had to remind me, "Take care of her. She is your dog."

I didn't like hearing those words—your dog. I wouldn't have minded the phrase "your dog to play with" or "your dog when you want her" or even " your dog when she is behaving. . . ." That's when it occurred to me. I am stuck with Liz. The courtship was over, the honeymoon had ended. We were mutually leashed. Liz went from an option to an obligation, from a pet to a chore, from someone to play with to someone to care for.

Perhaps you can relate. . . . Only instead of being reminded, "She is your dog," you're told, "he is your husband" or, "He is your child, parent, employee, boss, or roommate.[1] —*Max Lucado*

∞ Where will you turn when the honeymoon is over in your relationships?

∞ What happens when the person you once loved is now a chore?

∞ What will be your choice today?

14. Write out Jude 20-21.

∞ In what are you to keep yourself?

Choose this day what you will believe, whom you will serve, how you will live!

There came a time in my adult Christian life when I was faced with tough relationship choices. I had been hurt by a divorce, hurt by Christians, and hurt by the cold reality of a life that didn't turn out the way I had planned. I was mad at the world!

My inner turmoil led me to justify some very ugly actions that were certainly not appropriate for a Christian. I felt myself sink deeper and deeper into the pit of hate and despair. I was in agony. Then one day, a wise man gave me great advice. He looked me straight in the eyes and said, "I know you have been hurt, but your hurt will carry on in your children if you do not give it to God. Do you want your children to have a legacy of hate, hurt, and bitterness, or do you want to give them the legacy of love and forgiveness? You can't tell them about God's love if you aren't first walking in that love yourself."

I would like to say that I snapped out of my pain and that from that day on I behaved perfectly! But . . . you guessed it . . . that was not the case. I did, however, make a choice that day—a choice to open up every part of me to God for healing and wholeness. It was then that I began learning how part of being completely whole is learning what it means to live in God's love. The choice was mine, the power to heal and deliver was God's. Jesus met me at the crossroads of love and hate. And, as a result of His power working in me, I have experienced God doing the impossible in my heart of hearts. I praise God for the legacy of His love.

Father,

Sometimes I think it would be easier if I were a pre-programmed robot. But, in reality I am thankful that You made Your people capable of making choices. I desire to choose life in Your Spirit. Walking in Your love toward others is choosing life. It is a serious endeavor. For when I do not choose love and the walk of love, I am in darkness. Impress on my heart how important it is to love as I am loved. And, as each new challenge emerges, speak gently to my heart: "Child, you have a choice." Father, now empower me to make choices that will please You, by the mighty power of Your Spirit, who works in me to will and to do of Your good pleasure. Amen.

Living Love . . . As God Has Loved Us

"Since God so loved us, we also ought to love one another"
(1 John 4:11).

We all want to be treated fairly. When we are treated unfairly at the hands of another Christian, we are shocked and amazed. "This is not right," we say. "This is not how Christians should act!" Yet, the circle of unfairness goes round and round, as we too hurt others. We get sloppy with our words, we fail to protect those who belong to Christ, and we act in ways that are not pleasing to God. We are hurt when gossip is hurled at us, but we continue to talk about others, don't we? We are incensed when misunderstood, but are quick to pass judgment ourselves. Cover it up all you want, but the truth is—God sees it all!

Sometimes the way we treat others is just nonsense. Sadly, Christians are known to shoot their wounded. Christians can be rude, arrogant, exclusive, and unloving. Rather than being a vessel of peace and love, the church can often be a vessel of hurt and confusion. In a perfect world, we would all "get it" and understand the importance of loving one another. But we are not perfect—we are people, and people need the Lord.

God demonstrates His love to us everyday. He loves imperfect ones like you and me. Now, let's pray for the power to give God's love to others in the same way God freely gives it to us.

1. Read 1 John 4:16-21.

∞ What is God? (v. 16)

∞ In this world, whom are you to be like? (v. 17)

∞ Why do you love? (v. 19)

∞ What are you if you love God and hate others? (v. 20)

∞ Write out 1 John 4:21.

∞ Think of the "brothers" in your life—a spouse, child, parent, employee, boss, relative, or roommate. How does God want you to relate to these people in your life?

2. **Read 1 John 2:9-11 and rewrite this passage in your own words.**

> *Stumble:*
> *To lose one's footing*
> *To make a false step*
> *To lose balance*

We are fooling ourselves if we talk the great talk of faith in God, and then turn on those that God loves. Notice the word *stumble* here in this passage. When I walk in the light of God's love, there is nothing to make me stumble.

But, when I walk in hate and animosity toward another, I lose my balance in life. The word *hate* here comes from the Greek *miseo,* which means to detest, to persecute, to love less. The word *detest* can mean *dislike* and *hostility.* It is important to break down the meaning of this word because I think we fool ourselves by thinking, *I don't hate anyone!*

However, the truth is that even when we refuse to give people a chance, disliking them and judging them, we begin acting in a false way. We smile and behave as if everything is fine, while secretly disliking them. Then we lose our footing because in such a place we are actually in darkness. Sometimes in this place our false sense of being okay has blinded us, and we don't realize how far we have come from fellowship with God.

3. Write out Matthew 22:37-40.

No matter what your circumstances God has called you to two basics:

1. Love the Lord with every part of yourself;
2. Love others as you love yourself.

You may be thinking, *Love others as well as I love myself? You've gotta be kidding! I don't love myself. In fact, I have trouble even liking myself!*

Accepting and understanding God's love for us is so very important! Scripture doesn't say we are to spend hours and hours seeking to love ourselves. That would be self-absorption, and that is clearly not God's plan. But, we are to know God's Word and seek to understand the truth that it represents. We are continually to fill ourselves with His truth for us, to combat the lies of hell, the lies of our pasts, and the lies of the culture we live in. Stay in His Word. Pursue the truth of God's love. Then make it a pursuit of your life to extend that love to others. Remember, all of this is made possible by God's Spirit at work in us.

> Jesus said, "Love the Lord your God with all your passion and prayer and intelligence." This is the most important, the first on any list. But there is a second to set alongside it: "Love others as well as you love yourself." These two commands are pegs, everything in God's Law and the Prophets hangs from them (Matthew 22: 37–40, TM).

4. Read John 14:15-18.

∞ What did Jesus say He would do for you? (v. 16)

∞ What is the name of the Holy Spirit? (v. 17)

∞ Where is He at this very moment?

In John 14, Jesus was making it clear that He would be crucified. His followers didn't know what they would do once He went away. He had helped them so much, done many miracles, and made such a difference. They didn't want Him to die, to go away . . . they were afraid. But, in His loving way, Jesus told them not to be afraid (John 14:1). He told them to trust in God, and then He told them of the provision of God's Spirit.

> The Holy Spirit is God Himself, a person with whom you can enjoy a personal relationship. He is not merely an impersonal force or power or essence within the universe, but He is rather a person who can speak to you and to whom you can speak. He is a person who can guide you, who can help you, who can strengthen you, who can teach you the truth of God. . . . When Jesus told His disciples, "I will pray the Father, and He will give you another Helper, that He may abide with you forever" (John 14:16), He was encouraging His men to prepare for a new way in which God would thereafter be relating to them.[2]
> —*Chuck Smith*

God is calling us to live in a new way, and it will be accomplished by His Spirit.

5. **Write out Romans 12:9-10.**

∞ What are two stances that you are to take toward another person? (v. 10)

∞ Look up the following words in the dictionary and write down the definitions.
  • Devoted:

  • Honor:

The Bible doesn't instruct us just to love and honor those who are wonderful to us. In Romans 12, Paul tells us we are to bless those who curse us! Imagine someone telling you off, I mean really cursing at you, hurting you, and defaming your character. What does the Word of God tell you to do in such a situation? Bless 'em! Love 'em! Grace 'em! Yes that's right . . . we are to learn to walk in love because that is what God's Word tells us to do and because it pleases our Heavenly Father. This type of love-walk is accomplished by relationship with God and the empowering of the Holy Spirit. It's like picking up your rental car and finding out you have been upgraded. Instead of getting a small budget car (your human strength), you are given the keys to a spacious luxury car (the power of God's strength through His Spirit in you). Do you want to argue and insist on the budget car? Or, are you going to get excited and hop in the upgrade and paint the town? In much the same way, God is giving us more than we could ever afford for ourselves. He gives us the power of His Spirit. Are we going to argue and insist on keeping our puny strength and worn out effort, or are we going to take what He gives us?

6. **Read Ephesians 4:1-6.**
   ෨ Write out Ephesians 4:2.

   ෨ What are the key thoughts in this verse?

7. **Read Ephesians 4:17-23.**
   ෨ Write out Ephesians 4:23-24.

   ෨ According to these verses, what is to be made new?

   ෨ When embarking on any lifestyle change, what is the first thing to be changed?

   ෨ What is your part in a choice? (Refer to the "put on" part of the passage.)

   ෨ What is the new self supposed to look like?

8. **Read Ephesians 5:1-2.**
   ෨ Whom are you to imitate?

∞ How would this change your life and relationships with others?

We see the ideal and understand what God intended for us to be, and in our heart we desire to live a life of love and purity, righteousness, truth, and peace. But then somehow we imagine we can achieve that goal by sheer effort and brute resolve. Yet the mere desire to be like Jesus doesn't itself create the reality. It doesn't enable us to realize our goal. We do not become like Christ by imitation, which is where a lot of people go awry. Jesus once said to Peter after he had failed yet again, "The spirit indeed is willing, but the flesh is weak"(Matthew 26:41, KJV).

> *Therefore be imitators of God—copy Him and follow His example—as well-beloved children [imitate their father] (Ephesians 5:1, AMP).*

> I am certain that all of us have found this to be true in our own experience. We don't lack desire; it isn't that our spirit is unwilling. The problem is that our flesh is weak. That's why mere imitation will never work . . . God wants to conform us to the image of His Son. That's the work He is doing in our lives through the Spirit.[3]—*Chuck Smith*

9. Write out Romans 8:29.

∞ What work does God do in your life?

∞ How will this change you, making you more like Christ in love and life?

What a beautiful Helper the Holy Spirit is! And how we need His help to lead a successful Christian life. We need Him to indwell us, to lead us and empower us. We need His presence, we need His power, we need His leading. We need to walk in the Spirit so that we will not fulfill the lusts of our flesh. The flesh life is very strong; only God's Holy Spirit is stronger.[4]
—Chuck Smith

It is funny to me that even though we are Christians, we use the methods of the world, and its psychology to determine how we will "really" live, and how we will "really" find happiness. We have a preoccupation with ourselves, our feelings, and our rights. Many Christians are not convicted at all when they treat others poorly as long as they can justify themselves. This is not God's way, it is the way of the world. In Ephesians 5, we can clearly see that we are to:

Love,
Imitate God,
Put on the new self,
Find out what pleases the Lord.

Don't love the world's ways. Don't love the world's goods. Love of the world squeezes out love for the Father. Practically everything that goes on in the world—wanting your own way, wanting everything for yourself, wanting to appear important—has nothing to do with the Father. It just isolates you from him. The world and all its wanting, wanting, wanting is on the way out—but whoever does what God wants is set for eternity (1 John 2:15-17, TM).

10. Read 1 John 1:5-10.
∽ What does this passage say about sin?

∞ What is it saying regarding darkness and light in relationships?

∞ Do you have unloving areas in your life that you need to confess to God? What are they?

11. Write out Psalm 139:23-24.

> *If someone claims, "I know him well!" but doesn't keep his commandments, he's obviously a liar. His life doesn't match his words. But the one who keeps God's word is the person in whom we see God's mature love. This is the only way to be sure we're in God. Anyone who claims to be intimate with God ought to live the same kind of life Jesus lived (1 John 2:4-5, TM).*

This is how you should start each day if you are going to embark on the path of living God's love. It's like Wheaties for the soul. When kids have extra energy, we sometimes say, "They ate their Wheaties this morning!" Well, when you are loving despite the circumstances, it's because you were with God eating those spirtual Wheaties of:

Adoration—I worship You today, God.

Confession—I need You today, forgive me of my sins.

Thanksgiving—I thank You for every person and every thing in my life today.

Supplication—I pray for Your love in every relationship.

12. Write out the following two verses.
∞ Psalm 133:1:

∞ John 17:11:

It is clear that God has called us to live in unity and to live a life of love.

Throughout this study on *Living Love,* keep in mind our pattern of love is God Himself (1 Corinthians 13). It would be helpful to read and reread 1 Corinthians 13 each week as you are renewing your mind in God's way of living out His love. Pray and ask the Holy Spirit to conform you to the image of Jesus, working into your life the pattern of God's love.

In this list of *Love's Obstacles,* check the characteristics that generally apply to you in relationships. Then pray about them in the way that David prayed in Psalm 139:23-24.

LOVE'S OBSTACLES	
_____ Defensiveness	_____ Unforgiveness
_____ Anger	_____ Bitterness
_____ Pride	_____ Hatred
_____ Neediness	_____ Judgmental Attitude
_____ Stubbornness	_____ Jealousy
_____ Pain	_____ Competitiveness

Now, in this list of *Love's Pattern,* check those things that you need more of in your life. Ask the Holy Spirit to work in you.

LOVE'S PATTERN	
_____ Patience	_____ Not Self-Seeking
_____ Kindness	_____ Not Easily Angered
_____ Does Not Envy	_____ Keeps No Records of Wrongs
_____ Does Not Boast	_____ Protects
_____ Not Proud	_____ Trusts/Hopes
_____ Not Rude	_____ Perseveres

> Love is what we will show in our lives if we have got the love of God shed abroad in our hearts. We will not have to go up and down the earth proclaiming it. We will show it in everything we say or do.—*Author unknown*

Father,

I desire to know what it means to love as You have loved me. I want to walk in love as You did. Not some flimsy, shallow love, but, a real, abiding, authentic type of love. Oh, Jesus, I find this type of love so attractive, and my heart yearns to walk in a love that is not selfish and not looking for anything in return. Thank You for giving Yourself for me. Now may I learn to live to pour out and give myself for others. Fill me with Your love. Amen.

LIVING LOVE . . . WITH A NEW HEART

"The precepts of the Lord are right, giving joy to the heart"
(Psalm 19:8).

It happened suddenly and without warning—at sixty-eight my mother's heart stopped as she suffered a massive heart attack. The family cried and prayed, and a determined young doctor tried everything. Once again her heart began to find a rhythm. Though she was immediately placed on life support systems and suffered through a long recovery, she did live through that life-threatening attack. As she recovered in ICU, she was poked and prodded through test after test until the diagnosis was clear—her heart was destroyed. Then she was faced with a major dilemma: would she be willing to undergo major heart surgery? This was not a simple bypass because every feeder vein into her heart was blocked, the main arteries as well as all the small ones.

Through the hands of a skilled doctor, she underwent major surgery and survived a twelve-way bypass—a rare surgery indeed. It gave her many more years of life.

God was with her, He wasn't through with her yet . . . and He healed her heart—literally!

In much the same way, we too need a surgeon's touch on our hearts. I am not speaking of the heart muscle itself, but rather the heart of who we are. Jesus is the master surgeon who can unclog all of the arteries that lead to our heart of hearts. Our all-wise God can do spiritual surgery on the vessels that are clogged with things such as hurt, bitterness, misunderstanding, and unforgiveness.

Every person has a story. And usually that story has included some type of hurt and pain at the emotional level. Sometimes we get blocked or clogged in our personal pain. Even as Christian women, we are sometimes unwilling to yield certain parts of our hearts to God. We think that He will make us love people we hate, and like people we aren't interested in. Sometimes we just want to be left alone when it comes to relationships. But God has the way to health, and it is through living a life of love.

God has the power to heal our emotions and our hearts. As this tremendous healing takes place, we become free from fear, and we find ourselves becoming willing to love others with a new heart—the heart of Jesus.

This is a major breakthrough in our Christian lives. We need new hearts!

1. Read Ezekiel 11:14-21.

The book of Ezekiel is named after the prophet Ezekiel, whose name means *God is strong.* During his ministry Ezekiel proclaimed the same basic message as did Jeremiah—Jerusalem and the people in it were doomed because of the sinfulness of their hearts and their idolatry. In this passage he gives those that are far away from the Lord new hope. The hope of a new heart.

⬯ Do you ever feel as if your heart is divided between what you feel like doing and what you know God wants you to do?

⬯ As a Christian woman what do the words *undivided heart* mean to you?

2. Write out Ezekiel 11:19, personalizing it by writing your name in place of the word *them.*

∞ Now journal what this verse is saying to you and how it could be applied to your life today.

A woman with an undivided heart is a woman with singleness of heart. She has one purpose and that is to live for God. But we all are human flesh with hearts that have become hard, deaf, and sometimes as immovable as a stone. God gives us hope that He can and will give us a heart transplant. He will give us a new, tender heart that is receptive and responsive to God's Spirit. Do you need a heart transplant?

3. Read Jeremiah 32:37-41.

God is gracious to the woman who repents, isn't He? Repenting is when we turn away from our wrongdoing, our wrong attitudes, and our sin. We come to God and ask Him to forgive us, and then we turn in the direction He is leading. This direction for most of us is a complete, about face! A 180-degree spin!

∞ According to Jeremiah 32:39, what does God say He will give you when you turn back to Him?
Singleness of:

_____ and _____

In this Jeremiah passage we see the word *fear* in relation to our journey with God. This fear is the attitude of holy reverence. It is a fear that says: I must humble myself before Him because He is God, and because He can do as He wills. He is my maker, and I am His.

According to Jeremiah 32:39, why is it good to have a reverent fear of God?
For:

_____ and _____

∞ What does God "rejoice in doing" in your life? (v. 41)

4. Read Deuteronomy 5:29-32.
∞ What does verse 32 say you are to do?

∞ Write out the following verses.
- Deuteronomy 5:33

- John 13:34

∞ According to these two verses, what are you to walk in?

5. Read Deuteronomy 6:1-5.
∞ What does verse 2 say will be affected if you obey and serve the Lord?

If we believe the children are the future, isn't it wise to raise them God's way? Too often we teach them a double standard. We talk about love, and we don't live in love. They are not stupid.

Your children will follow your lead. If you are unkind, critical, and have a tendency to gossip, they will follow that pattern. As they get older, they will wonder how your Christian faith and your hard heart coexist! Isn't it time to get serious before God about our lives and our hearts?

6. Write out John 4:23-24.

☙ According to this passage, how are you to worship and live before God?

Do you ever fall into the trap of living by appearances only? People see the heart we have painted on us. They don't see the real heart, but God does. And He sees us through eyes of love and compassion. He desires to give us a new heart so that we can live for Him in honesty, worshiping in spirit and in truth. In so doing, we will be affecting lives all around us.

7. **Read Deuteronomy 6:4-9.**
☙ Write out verse 5.

☙ Read Matthew 22:34-40.
☙ According to Scripture, what is the most important thing in life?

☙ What is the second most important thing?

8. **Write out Deuteronomy 6:7.**

☙ What are you to impress on your children?

☙ How do you think that is accomplished?

☙ Do your children see the real you behind closed doors?

∞ Could you use a new heart and a right spirit? Why?

9. Read 2 Corinthians 5:7-10.
∞ How do these verses tell you to live?

∞ What should be your main goal in life?

∞ Does living in God's love please Him? How?

10. Write out 2 Corinthians 5:14-15.

∞ For whom are we to live?

Ouch! So much of the time I just live for me. I attend my own pity parties, crying in my own root beer and hardening my heart with mountains that I have made out of molehills! Can you relate?

But as Christ's love compels me, influencing me in the right direction, I become more and more convinced that the right way to live is *for Him.* This is huge when applied to all interpersonal relationships. Now, I can let go of the small stuff that normally would send me over the edge. I become healed in my heart, and this affects my personality and my actions toward others.

11. Read 2 Corinthians 5:16-21.
∞ How are you to stop looking at people?

∞ What ministry did God give to you?

∞ What message has been committed to you?

∞ In verse 20 of this passage, what are you called?

We are representing Christ in this world—that is what the Christian life is about. But, because we think it is all about "us," we get off track. Let's look at this idea of representation, or being ambassadors of Christ. We are to represent God, and God is love—this is the nature of who God is. Jesus Christ His Son was sent to the world in God's love so that no one would perish. The very essence of who Jesus Christ is, is love.

The message of reconciliation is the message of God's love for His people. His appeal is that of love. What are we doing then . . . living for ourselves, with hearts that are hardened to the people around us? We can sing a song, speak a praise, lift our hands, but are we God's ambassadors of love?

The most natural way to see someone is from a worldly point of view. What we see is what we get, mixed with our own perceptions of who someone is. We see here in 2 Corinthians that we are no longer to look just at what we see, but instead to look at people as those Christ loves. In order to do this we need a new heart.

12. Read Isaiah 61:1-7.

These verses speak of a people who are transformed by Jesus Christ. People formerly devastated, living in the midst of ancient ruins, now being restored, rebuilt, and renewed. Maybe you are living in the rubble of ancient ruins too. Your heart may need to be rebuilt and renewed. God, through Jesus, makes beautiful things of our hearts and lives as we submit ourselves to Him. Just look at some of the things He does for you, according to Isaiah 61:1-7.

- He preaches good news to your poor tired heart.
- He binds up the broken places in your heart.
- He proclaims that you can be free from the captivity of the negative impact of relationships.

- He releases you from darkness and from your prison of hate—through His Word.
- He comforts you as you cry and process some of the pain of life.
- He crowns you with beauty as He takes you out of the ashes.
- He anoints you with joy and gladness as He lifts you from your mourning.
- He wraps you in a new garment of praise, instead of your rags of despair.
- He calls you an oak of righteousness and displays splendor through you.
- He declares that you are His planting, so you can have confidence and bloom in His love.
- He rebuilds, restores, and renews you! Everlasting joy will be yours!

Wow! How wonderful that God provides all we need to live with new hearts.

As we continue to study, we will look at some areas that can clog the arteries if we are not careful to walk in His ways.

Let's stop right now, and thank God for who He is and for the new heart He desires to give us. Today put on your Jesus glasses, and begin looking at life and love through a new lens. Take a good look at those you come in contact with, looking at them through your Jesus glasses, your new eyes of love. You will be surprised how refreshing it is to see people with God's eyes, viewing them from His viewpoint and loving them because they are His.

You are God's representative. In order to represent Him, you must know Him. In the business world, a sales representative knows the product and knows the manufacturer's goals and targets in marketing/representing it to the public. In the same way, we are to know Him and acquaint ourselves with His goals. We then move and live in those goals because we are representing Him. His goal is love, and in Isaiah 61, we can see how that love is played out in practical ways in our lives. Let's go forward with new hearts, tender hearts, willing hearts, yielded hearts . . . to love Him, and love others.

Go !

Father,

I need Your heart! So many things have hurt me, and so much junk is piled high in my heart that I am surprised it can even keep beating. I ask You to replace all hardness in my heart, in relation to Your will or Your Word. Replace it with a willingness to love others and to serve You. And, replace it with Your warm, caring, honest heart. I love You Lord, and it is my desire to be called a minister of God as I represent You in my little corner of the world. Be glorified in me! Amen.

Living Love . . . Despite our Hurts

Love is the soy sauce on the chop suey of life.

Everyone will experience hurt in this lifetime. You don't have to be a genius to figure that out. In fact, you don't have to go far to find hurting, needy people. Usually that person is as close as your own mirror. Who is she? Where has she been? How have life's hurts affected the image looking back at her?

We can put on a smile, cover up the redness of eyes spent with tears, but within our hearts we know far too well that the hurts that have come our way have changed us. For some the changes have been for the better. For others the change has produced a bitter and defensive woman who is hard on the inside despite her outward loveliness.

Hurts come in many shapes and sizes. Hurts can harm us, or help us. What will your choice be? Your personal hurt can be the stepping stone to becoming a more mature woman, or it can be the tombstone that kills you with anger and bitterness. You can get bitter, or you can get better!

1. Read Psalm 15.

According to this psalm, the one who is blameless and does what is righteous also does what else?

1.

2.

3.

4.

5.

6.

7.

8.

9.

Righteous people keep their oath even when it hurts. Wow! Is this contrary to the world's way of handling things. The last verse of Psalm 15 makes it clear that we will not be shaken when we keep on trusting, but rather we will walk uprightly, even when it hurts. Keep your commitment to God, and your commitment to living in love, even when it hurts.

> There is only one being who loves perfectly, and that is God, yet the New Testament distinctly states that we are to love as God does; so the first step is obvious. If ever we are going to have perfect love in our hearts we must have the very nature of God in us. In Romans 5:5 the Apostle Paul tells us how this is possible; he says "the love of God is shed abroad in our hearts by the Holy Ghost which is given unto us." He is speaking not of the power to love God, but the very love of God itself which is "shed abroad"—a superabounding word, it means that the love of God takes possession of every crook and cranny of our nature.[1]—*Oswald Chambers*

2. **Write out Psalm 71:20-21.**

> *Humble yourselves,*
> *therefore, under*
> *God's mighty hand,*
> *that he may lift you*
> *up in due time. Cast*
> *all your anxiety on*
> *him because he*
> *cares for you*
> *(1 Peter 5:6–7).*

∞ What can God do even after you have been hurt or grown bitter?

∞ Write out the dictionary definition of *restore.*

I like the synonym of *restore*—to renew and revive. God has the power to renew and revive you even though you have been hurt by someone. First, we must follow the scriptural example and start by giving the burden of the hurt to God.

3. **Look up the following verses, making notes on the key point of each passage.**
   • Psalm 55:22

   • Psalm 60:11

   • Psalm 61:2

   • Psalm 62:8

   • Psalm 68:19-20

4. Write out Psalm 25:21.

David had enemies on every side. Yet, through it all he learned to lean on God and trust in God's unfailing love. Do you generally look to God through your hurts, or do you try to handle the situation on your own? I would say that probably most women try to fix things before giving them to God or following in His way.

Honestly . . . how do you usually respond when someone hurts you? Mark the characteristics that apply to your response.

_____ get angry

_____ fume

_____ become defensive

_____ plot to make offender see error

_____ gossip about offender

_____ turn others against offender

_____ act kindly despite offender's problem

_____ cry

_____ give silent treatment

_____ fight back inside

_____ think of ways to get even

_____ throw Scripture at offender

_____ sulk

_____ seek revenge

_____ trust God to handle offender

_____ eat

_____ pray for God to bless offender

_____ turn the other cheek

5. Read Ephesians 4:1-3.

∞ What is Paul urging you to do here?

1. Live_____

2. Be_____

3. Be_____

4. Make_____

∞ Read Philippians 2:3-8.

∞ Do you usually look after only your own interest in an argument, or do you have the other person's heart and life in mind too? Explain.

Our selfishness and shortsightedness will cause us to act in *opposition* to the flow of God's Spirit if we do not watch out. Keep yourself on a short

leash, so to speak, when it comes to your dealing
with others who have hurt you. Do not defend
yourself, do not be proud and vain. Ask God to
empower you to quit thinking life is only about
you and what "that person did to *me*." If we are to
be lifted to new heights in our walk with God, we
must learn to follow in His ways, even when doing
so is hard, uncomfortable, or unnatural. Sometimes I feel as if God is saying, "Debbie, get over yourself!"

> We are to do noth-
> ing out of:
> selfish ambition
> or
> vain conceit.

6. Write out Romans12:14.

∞ What are you to do to people who hurt you?

∞ What are you not to do?

BLESS:	CURSE:
to honor	to cause harm
to pray for	to cause evil to befall upon
to ask for divine favor for	to swear at in profane terms
to confer well being or prosperity upon	to wish ill well and bad luck upon

> To love people we don't like is one of life's great challenges. It
> takes extra motivation and help from outside ourselves. For me,
> the greatest motivation to love people I don't like is God's love
> for me. When we struggle in our response to another person,

we must remember that we are all sinners whom God has forgiven for many things. If we can not forgive others for their sins
against us, then perhaps we have lost sight of just how much
we have been forgiven.[2]—*Floyd McClung, Jr.*

7. **Read Romans 12:17-21.**

∞ Write out Romans 12:17.

We need to get this ingrained in our minds. Payback is not God's will
for His people. Prayer, not payback, is the way to win the war in hurtful
relationships. This is such an important truth and guideline. It is easier to
just lash out or resort to our unhealthy forms of communication and problem solving when someone hits us where it hurts. But **we must NOT!**
Payback is not God's way.

Are you feuding with a friend, family member, coworker, or ex-spouse?
Do not pay back the hurt this person caused you; it will only end up
destroying you, and it is contrary to the way God would have you spend
your time and energy. Remember, the way God desires us to spend our time
and energy is in learning how to love Him with all of our being, and then
to love others.

8. **Write out Romans 12:16 and 18.**

∞ What do these verses tell you to do in your relationships?

∞ Do you think peace is always possible? Explain.

Obviously, it is not always possible for things to go smoothly in relationships. You, however, are only responsible for *your part* of the relationship—the Bible says "as far as it depends on you, live at peace with everyone" (Romans 12:18). Many times I am the one who keeps the fire of hassle burning. I run swiftly to old methods of handling hurts. Sometimes I sulk, and other times I storm. And usually it is all because of my own pride! Sometimes it is because the hurt brings out an old insecurity that needs to be healed and made secure and whole by God's touch.

Don't waste time concentrating on blaming others. Sure, maybe they did something awful, but now, what are you going to do with their awful behavior? Could it be happening so that you can understand yourself better, seek God more, and learn to love more fully?

9. **Read Romans 12:16.**
   This verse tells you two things you are not to be:
   Do not be _____, and
   do not be _____.

Sounds familiar, like the "selfish ambition and vain conceit" we looked at earlier. Selfishness causes many problems in our relationships. Selfishness causes us to hold on to hurts and offenses so tightly that our white-knuckled grasp can hardly be broken.

I can not live in harmony if I am full of myself . . . full of pride. In this position I end up thinking everything needs to go my way or revolve around me. When I think too highly of myself, I am not humble before my Heavenly Father, and I can not hear the voice of God or the Spirit's direction in the middle of the hurt. Laying my life before the Father is necessary if I am going to learn to love despite the hurts that are hurled at me.

> **Selfish:**
> *Concerned only or primarily with oneself or one's own interest.*
> *Not much regard for others*
> *Self-seeking*
> *Self-centered*

Selfishness is obviously contrary to God's ways. Love is not self-seeking and is not proud. Love also holds others in honor and high regard because it rejoices in the truth, protects, and hopes for the best in another's life.

Revenge:
*to impose or inflict
injury in turn for
injury*

10.   Write out Romans 12:19.

11.Read Romans 12:20.

∞ How are you to treat an enemy or someone who has hurt you?

12. Write out Romans 12:21. Memorize this verse. This is good 3 x 5 card material!

How do you suppose you can overcome evil with good? What are some practical ways that you can turn the other cheek or overcome the evil in a situation?

13. Read James 5:13-18.

This passage speaks of what to do when the rubber meets the road, or when your relationships hit the wall! There are many different ways we can deal with hurts. The choice we make in dealing with our hurts will affect the outcome. If we want to overcome evil, then we must *carefully* choose our way of handling people and situations. There is a saying, "Life is precious, handle with prayer." Well, life and people are both precious. We should pray until something happens! Elijah prayed earnestly, and what happened? (vv. 17-18)

In every situation we have the following options:

1. Internalize and become bitter.

2. Pay back and try to get even.

3. Forgive and hand things over to Jesus.

Internalize

This is a game of pretend and pretense. When we grit our teeth, suck it all up, paste a happy smile on our face, we are only allowing the problem to go unresolved, making room for resentment and bitterness to grow. This way of handling an offense only allows us to become a pressure cooker ready to blow at the next slightest offense. Often we feel as if God isn't concerned with our little hurts so we try to hang on for dear life with our own strength. This does not work. We must cast our cares, hurts, worries, and fears on God because He cares for us (1 Peter 5:7).

If you choose, *and yes it is a choice*, to internalize your hurts, holding tightly to them, you are allowing those hurts to sour your personality and all that God has created you to be. How can you have a countenance of joy and faith when you are harboring resentment and simmering in a pot of bitterness? You may also end up battling the hurdle of depression because depression is anger turned inward.

Payback

We all know how to do this. I don't care if you are the most "spiritual" woman in the church, given the right fuel for the fire you know exactly how to pay others back for the hurt they have caused you. Remember, we are all imperfect flesh, and when we walk in the flesh, we will fulfil its lusts and passions. Paying back is walking in the flesh, and not in the Spirit.

Sometimes we silently pay back by holding a grudge against others. We foolishly think that our grudge will hurt them. What's really happening is that the offender is living "rent free" in our minds and harassing our every waking thought! Our offenders could probably care less what we think right now so our payback will not impress or affect them.

God's way is to love them, do good to them. Give a soft and gentle answer to their anger, and the Bible says that will turn away wrath (Proverbs 15:1). You will probably not get instant results, but as you persevere, you will see God's faithfulness. Now, isn't that better than payback?

> When they hurled insults at him, he did not retaliate; when he suffered, he made no threats. Instead, he entrusted himself to him who judges justly (1 Peter 2:23).

Forgive

> They called him every name in the book and he said nothing back. He suffered in silence, content to let God set things right (1 Peter 2:23, TM).

Forgiveness is key in a Christian walk. Forgiveness is not forgetting that the offense happened, but it is giving it up and letting it go. This is much easier said than done, but we can do all things through Christ who has given us the strength to obey His Word and follow in His way (Philippians 4:13).

You may never get an apology from people who have hurt you. That's okay. Despite others' actions, you can be freed by examining your own heart, owning your own feelings of hurt and anger, and asking God to work in the very heart of you and give you the ability and will to let go and trust Him.

Do you really want other's offenses to rule your life? You can wait for the apology that may never come or you can ask God to show you His way of walking in love with people. Forgiveness is one of the keys that unlocks us and keeps our hurts from destroying our personality, health, and other relationships. Forgiveness is the antidote for the poison that begins brewing when we are wronged. Forgiveness is possible when you process through the pain of your hurt in light of God's Word, committing yourself and your feelings to God. You then move into a choice that makes His Word and His will the focus of your healing.

> For it is commendable if a man bears up under the pain of unjust suffering because he is conscious of God (1 Peter 2:19).

The key behind forgiveness is:
being conscious of God (WWJD?), and
being content to let God set things right.

> Do not conform any longer to the pattern of this world, but be transformed by the renewing of your mind (Romans 12:2).

The moment we start hating others, we become their slaves. When we obsess over wrongs done to us we become more conscious of the wrongs that have come our way, than the good that God brings into our lives. In this place we can't enjoy life the way we previously did, and we are plagued with angry thoughts, sour rumblings of the mind, and often physical symptoms. We may have trouble sleeping or eating. Some of us may fall into depression or sleep and eat too much! All the while those who hurt us are living their lives and doing their own thing. Doesn't it make more sense to submit to God and follow in God's way of love?

Doing things God's way will require a lifestyle change because it does not come naturally to our flesh nature. A lifestyle change happens when your mind is renewed (Romans 12:2).

This verse means that when we put new ideas and truth into our minds over and over, our lives will begin to take on a new belief system, and our actions will follow our beliefs and new values.

From the time we were children, we learned to act in self-defense. As we grew to be adults, we were taught that it is important to stand up and be counted and defend ourselves. We are now told even as Christians that we must watch out for ourselves because nobody else will. Tell me, where is this principle found in Scripture?

> *You who are servants, be good servants to your master—not just to good masters, but also to bad ones. What counts is that you put up with it for God's sake when you're treated badly for no good reason. This is the kind of life you've been invited into, the kind of life Christ lived. He suffered everything that came his way so you would know that it could be done, and also know how to do it, step by step* (1 Peter 2:18, 20 TM).

Of course, someone will watch out for me! My Heavenly Father already knows what I need. He sees every offense, He knows my frame, and the frame of my offenders. He can do incredibly more for me than I can do by watching out for myself because He is a big and mighty and powerful God!

In the Company of Roses

Roses are grown for the Vienna market in great profusion and with much distillation of fragrance. We are told that if you were to visit that valley at the time of the rose crop, wherever you would go the rest of the day, the fragrance you would carry with you would betray where you had been.

There is a beautiful parable given to us by the Persian

poet, Saadi. The poet was given a bit of ordinary clay. The clay was so redolent with sweet perfume that its fragrance filled all the room.

"What are you, musk or ambergris?" he questioned.

"I am neither" it answered. "I am just a bit of common clay."

"From where then do you have this rare perfume?" the poet asked.

"I have companied all the summer with a rose," it replied.

"We are just bits of the common clay of humanity. But if we company with the One who is the Rose of Sharon . . . something of the fragrance of His life will pass into ours. Then we will be a freshening and a sweetening influence to the world around us."³—*Henry Gariepy*

I have set before you life and death, blessings and curses. Now choose life, so that you and your children may live and that you may love the Lord your God, listen to his voice, and hold fast to him. For the Lord is your life, and he will give you many years in the land (Deuteronomy 30:19).

Your hurts can make you a *better* woman, or a *bitter* woman.

With whom will you keep company when in the middle of life's hurts?

Will you choose the sweet fragrance of Jesus today?

Father,

I don't want to be a bitter woman. But, sometimes relationships leave a sour taste, and I don't know what to do when everything within me wants revenge and payback. So now, I submit myself to You, and ask You, by the power of Your Spirit to put within me the desire to walk in Your way, and to give all of my hurts to You—You can take charge of them. I also give all of "me" to You—and You can take charge of me. Make me a lover of God and a lover of people. Amen.

LIVING FORGIVENESS . . . TRUE FREEDOM

Love is never letting a problem to be solved become more important than a person to be loved.

I will never forgive him!" As tears streamed down my new friend's face, falling onto her pale green sweater, I knew that though forgiveness was the last thing she wanted to face, it was the exact thing she finally needed to face—head on with Christ.

Forgiveness is a word that plants fear into the hearts of many people. We fear that if we forgive, we will be opening up ourselves for future hurt and mistreatment. Many of us feel that if we forgive others, it will be like letting them off the hook, or giving them a stamp of approval for the way they have wronged us.

Even Christians feel this way, and we struggle to believe that it is okay to let go and let God be God in all areas of our lives. Unfortunately what we fail to recognize is that when we as Christians insist on not forgiving, we are not living in God's best purpose for our lives. By not letting someone off the hook, we are actually snagging ourselves with that same hook and breeding bitterness, resentment, and all kinds of ugly things in our own hearts.

When bitterness reigns in our lives, we become negative, critical women. This kind of woman is not what God intended when He created us and when He forgave us in our own sinfulness. In many churches this type of woman is the norm. Sadly, we have become accustomed to judging one another harshly for every wrong performance.

God in His grace forgives us time and time again. Some of us have done ugly, hideous things, yet God forgives us over and over. Some of our hearts are full of deceitfulness and pride, yet God keeps loving us and working with us. One aspect of God's love toward us is forgiveness. And, He has clearly told us that we are to love as He has loved us (John 15:12). This is hard, if not impossible in most cases. But, with God all things are possible, and in Him we have strength for all things (Luke 1:37 and Philippians 4:13).

In this chapter we will look into God's Word and see what God's plan of forgiveness is for us in our relationships with other people.

1. **Read Matthew chapter 6:1-15.**

These are the words of Christ. Jesus is telling us some important life principles in this passage. We need to make note of some key points in this passage.

- We are not to do the right things for the sake of appearance and to please others. (What does Jesus call those who do this?)
- We are to remember that our Heavenly Father sees all things, even those things done in secret. We are to do all things unto Him, out of a heart of love for God.
- We must remember that our Heavenly Father knows our needs.
- We are to pray for God's will daily.
- We are to seek forgiveness from God for our sins, and we are to seek to forgive others as well.
- If we do not forgive, God will not forgive us.

Think about the intensity of what Jesus is saying here.

2. **Write out Matthew 6:14-15.**

Forgive here in the Greek language (*aphiemi*) can be translated as follows: forsake, lay aside, leave, let go, let alone, omit, yield up, put away. This definition speaks something powerful to me.

If I let go of the terrible things that someone has done to me, God will also let go of my offenses. Letting go means that I will choose to lay the offense aside and give it to God. Then God who sees in secret and knows my heart will honor me with the blessing of forgiving me too.

If I choose instead to hold on to the awful things done to me, then I will be guilty of not obeying the will of God. Instead, I will be holding tightly to my own will—my own hurts and my own perceived rights. When I live as one not yielding my life situations to my Heavenly Father, I am setting myself up for pain and separation from God.

My God knows and sees all things; therefore, I must live to please Him. If instead of pleasing God, I choose to please myself by nursing a grudge, I will also be choosing the consequences of that grudge. (Grudges happen when you don't lay aside wounds and let go of them.) Besides driving myself crazy with ugly thoughts and feelings, the worse consequence of my lack of submission to God and His Word is that I will not be forgiven for the wrongs that I commit.

∞ What does the Lord's prayer as outlined in Matthew 6, say to you on a personal level?

To forgive is also translated as *yield up*. It is important for us to realize that in our natural selves, we will have a very hard time forgiving someone who has hurt us. Sometimes we have a hard time forgiving someone even the smallest, petty offense. This is why it is important that we are aware that when God asks us to do something, His grace will enable us to carry it out. We must get in the habit of yielding up our hurts and offenses to God. Our Father who sees in secret will speak to the places in our hearts that need the strength of God in order to obey His Word. He will also give us personal and practical applications and steps to take in each individual circumstance. When . . . and IF . . . we yield to God.

3. **Read James 4:6-10.**
∞ What does God give you?

∞ What are three things you are to do? (vv.7-8)

1.

2.

3.

∞ What does "humble yourselves before the Lord" mean to you in the area of forgiving others for the things they have done to hurt you?

∞ Write out the dictionary definition of *humble*.

In the Greek translation of James 4:10 *humble* means to bring ourselves low, in the condition of our heart before God, to abase ourselves before God. One of the definitions in my dictionary reads: to take down a peg. I like that because that's exactly what I need to do in order to forgive someone. I must first get humble before my God— take myself down a peg—and look at the Lord God, His Word, and His ways. Then I can submit myself to His power and His word. Without this first step of humbling myself before Almighty God, I just might think someone actually owes me.

I find it quite interesting that the Bible tells us that the condition of our hearts should be to lower ourselves. The world says we are to elevate ourselves. Part of the reason it is so hard for us to let go and yield to God is because it has become unnatural for us to do so. The natural thing for us to do is to repay someone who has wronged us. We live in a get-in-your-face society. Sometimes we just want those who have hurt us to taste the pain we have tasted because of the way they mistreated us or those we love. But, in yielding to the natural, we set ourselves up for more pain. We do need, however, to confess the natural us to God—the real us (the us He already knows). When our hearts are laid open before Him, and we are no longer stuffing and brooding, we can instead begin confessing and be cleansed. Then we are in position to learn what it means to walk in the Spirit, rather than to walk in the old, natural patterns of our flesh.

Remember that God is love. He loves us and doesn't require anything of us that will ultimately harm us. His requirements bring us to a place of more wholeness and more peace. Everything we are looking for can be found in our Savior, and His ways for our lives.

4. **Read Matthew 18:21-35.**

∞ According to this passage, how many times did Jesus say you are to lay aside an offense and forgive?

∞ Do you ever tire of the same people doing hurtful things in your life? Explain.

∞ Do you tire of someone doing the same thing over and over? Describe one specific example.

> The key that opens the door to the locked rooms of our hearts is forgiveness. It is only when we have experienced forgiveness (and I cannot empasize strongly enough that I am not talking about the simple nodding of one's head to a preacher's words; I mean being overwhelmed by the reality of forgiveness, being able to touch, taste, and smell its results) that we find the locks are sprung, the doors flung open, the windows tossed high, the rooms inhabited, and fires lighted on the hearths. It is then we discover that our hearts are finally free to love. They have become what the Creator intended them to be, places with immense capacity to embrace. We may even hear ourselves saying with surprise, "Do you know, there isn't anyone I can't love!" Then we will discover that God had done his work in us.[1]
> —*Karen Burton Mains*

It is a natural response to rise up in self-defense when someone hurts us. But, just because it's natural to get defensive doesn't mean it's what is best for us. What's natural to us is usually just what is comfortable to our flesh or what is a natural pattern we have been taught to live by. As Christian women we are moving on to live in the Spirit, and what was once normal to us may suddenly seem the opposite of what God is calling us to live in now.

∞ According to Matthew 18:21-35 what did Jesus tell Peter he was to do when his friend/brother sinned against him?

∞ What about the person who just keeps on making the same mistake?

∞ Have you ever been like the wicked servant, wanting to squeeze out every bit of repayment from someone who unjustly wronged you? Briefly describe a situation.

Most of us can handle relationships when things are going well. We have no trouble responding to people who are being nice to us and who are meeting our expectations. It's when they don't do what we think is acceptable that we begin to lose our composure and often resort to acting according to our own natural flesh. We want to throw people in prison—the prison of revenge and hurt. When you forgive, you set the prisoner free. One of the definitions of forgive is *to give up wanting payback*. To forgive is to unlock the prison door and let the offender go free. But actually, the person you end up freeing the most is yourself.

"I have no choice." I often hear these words when someone is describing a painful situation in his life. Usually, the person sees himself as a helpless victim of evil persons or circumstances. In addition, depression, despair, and doubt characterize his thought life. Perhaps most damaging is a profound sense of powerlessness coloring his perspective. May I lovingly remind us that the powerless perspective is diametrically opposed to the Gospel of Jesus Christ? We possess incredible potential for choice and change! Why? Because the person who spoke the universe into existence offers to live within our beings. He has given us the power to choose Him as Lord of our entire lives, thus releasing new possibilities, perspectives, and power. And most amazing of all, this power to choose is available to every person! No exceptions! THE CHOICE IS OURS.[2] —*Steve Bearden*

5. **Write out 1 Corinthians 13:5. (Remember that the word it refers to love.)**

According to this verse, what four things are the opposite of God's love?
1.
2.
3.
4.

Make note this time of the fact that love does not keep record of wrongs.

We are to forgive over and over if that is what it takes. We can only do this when our eyes are fixed on Jesus, and we are lined up with the desires of the Holy Spirit. We must remember that forgiveness is a process of the heart. God is interested in the heart of us being yielded over to Him. Sometimes it doesn't feel at all black and white. In these times, we need to work through the gray areas with God—He will be faithful to lead us to the truth of forgiveness and love.

6. **Read Colossians 3. (The Rules for Holy Living)**
∞ According to Colossians 3:5 what in your life needs to die?

Put a checkmark by the following descriptions that apply to your earthly nature.

_____ having to have my own way
_____ being unwilling to obey God
_____ seeking revenge and repayment
_____ harboring anger, rage, and malice

∞ What is the new self being renewed in? (Colossians 3:10)

7. **What is Colossians 3:12-17 saying to you about your relationships with others?**

So, chosen by God for this new life of love, dress in the wardrobe God picked out for you: compassion, kindness, humility, quiet strength, discipline. Be even-tempered, content with second place, quick to forgive an offense. Forgive as quickly and completely as the Master forgave

∞ What do these verses say you are you to clothe yourself in?

∞ Where do you get these new garments?

8. **Write out Colossians 3:13. Memorize this verse!**

Forgiveness is lining your will up with God's Word and will. It is saying, Thy will be done! No one ever feels like forgiving. We cannot wait until we feel like forgiving. We usually aren't jumping for joy or ready to do things that are hard. We must acknowledge that we can forgive with God's strength, power, and love. We make the choice to obey God, He provides the power to complete the work. He does in us what we could never do ourselves.

> *you. And regardless of what else you put on, wear love. It's your basic, all-purpose garment. Never be without it (Colossians 3:12–14, TM).*

9. **Write out the following verses.**
   • Psalm 17:10:

   • Ephesians 4:18:

Has your heart become calloused because of an offense suffered? How do you think it happened?

In fact our recovery and well being is intimately tied to our forgiveness of others. It does no good to receive grace with one hand, and deal out judgement with the other (Matthew 18:21-35) We need to forgive not just with our will but from the "heart," from our whole being. Forgiveness is a deeply emotional process whereby we deal with all our feelings. We must be honest about our hurt and anger and not close our hearts and become callous.[3]—*Dr. Henry Cloud and Dr. John Townsend*

---

10. Read 1 Corinthians 10:13.
∞ Are you tempted today with unforgiveness? Why?

∞ What does 1 Corinthians 10:13 promise you?

On a piece of paper make a list of those whom you are holding captive in your mind due to the ill feelings of hurt, anger, or unforgiveness. If necessary, you may find it helpful to write a letter to each of these people. This letter will never be sent; it is for your healing and cleansing. Once the letter is written and your frustration is out in the open, pray. Then take your list and your letters and rip them up, burn them in a fireplace, or find a way to discard of them. This is symbolic of how you are handing these people and their offenses toward you over to God. They are in God's hands. He has provided a way of escape, and it is the love of Jesus.

It is God's will that you forgive your offenders; therefore, when you strongly do not want to act according to God's will, you are being tempted to follow your sinful human flesh, obeying the natural way of responding and doing things. If we are going to be lifted to new heights, we must follow God and obey His Word. It is an act of will and an act of choice, but the carrying out of that choice is a miracle of His Spirit. He desires to grant you that power, that miracle, that wonderful ability to:

rise above,

take the higher road,

walk in the Spirit,

turn the other cheek,

allow God to handle the offender.

God provides a way out, His word promises that.

11. Read Ephesians 4:30-32.
∞ According to these verses, what grieves the Holy Spirit?

∞ What are you to get rid of?

∞ How are you to live?

12. **Read Luke 6: 27-38. (An enemy is anyone you are at odds with today.)**
    Enemy: a hostile force, power, or person.
    According to this passage, we are to do these four things in our rela-
    tionships:
    love,
    bring good to,
    bless,
    pray for.

∞ Does this just apply to the good relationships? Explain. (Luke 6:32)

∞ How are you to treat those who actually hate you or cause you pain?
(Luke 6:28)

∞ Is this an impossible command or challenge? Why or why not?
(Philippians 4:13)

∞ In which of your relationships can you begin applying God's Word
today?

13. **We often are judgmental toward the difficult people in our lives. What
    does Luke 6:37 say we are not to do to these people?**
    • I am not to . . .

- I am not to . . .

∞ What are the two things in Luke 6:37-38 that you are to do in your relationships?

∞ Will you be blessed if you follow in God's ways? How?

∞ Journal your thoughts here.

Pray this week for each person you have had a difficult time loving or forgiving. Ask God to forgive you for holding on to the offense instead of yielding it up to Him. Pray according to God's Word. Ask God by the power of His Spirit to give you practical ideas and insights unique to your individual situation that will help you step out in a love-walk. Now that you have forgiven, ask God to continue working in the deepest parts of you. Walk by faith now, not by sight or feeling.

Remember, this does not mean you will forget the offense. You cannot forget a rape, death, abuse, divorce, adultery, theft, etc. But, the memory of an offense can lose its power, and the circumstance that has caused you hurt can be covered in Christ.

Only the Spirit of God could do such a wonderful work of grace and forgiveness in us. We just have to choose which direction we will go. To forgive or not to forgive is our decision. The choice we make determines the direction, God's grace and power determines the outcome.

We aren't aiming for a perfect performance, but we are making it our aim to be pointed in the right direction. In these situations the right direction is straight toward the heart of God, and His Word. When pointed in the direction of love, God can and will do amazing miracles in our hearts.

Trials are not enemies of faith
but are opportunities to see
the faithfulness of God.

Father,

It is my heart's desire to walk a walk worthy of the calling You have called me to. You have called me to be Your daughter, and now I want to live with Your eyes, seeing people the way You see them. I want to reflect the attitude and personality of my Father. And, I know that only You can do that perfect work in me. My part is to move closer to You through obedience, surrender, and humility. I am Yours Lord . . . all that I am, all that I will ever be. Teach me how to live. Amen.

LIVING MERCY . . .
AS HE IS MERCIFUL

Mercy is kind and compassionate treatment, coupled with a disposition toward forgiveness.

To have a disposition of forgiveness means that a person has a habitual tendency toward forgiveness. Such a person is inclined to offer forgiveness when needed. This is someone who is kind, compassionate, and merciful. Sounds to me like a sketch of God! Kindness, compassion, and mercy are all characteristics of Jesus Christ. If we are serious about learning to follow Him, we must seriously desire to understand these traits.

1. **Write out the following verses.**
   - Deuteronomy 4:31:

   - Nehemiah 9:31:

∞ What do these verses tell you about God?

2. **Write out Ephesians 2:4-6.**

↶ According to this passage of Scripture, what have God's love and mercy done for you?

↶ Do you act as though you are in Christ? Explain.

3. **Read Luke 6:32-36.**
↶ What does Jesus instruct you to do in these verses that can be applied to your everyday life?

↶ What characteristic of God does Jesus tell you to imitate? (v. 36)

4. **Read Luke 6:37-38.**
↶ A merciful person is someone who is Christlike . . . kind and forgiving. How does judging fit into the picture of a merciful person?

↶ Do you think someone oozing with mercy would be a critical and judgmental person? Why or why not?

↶ What measure will be used to you?

We live in a world of double standards. We judge others by a yardstick of perfect expectations, yet we don't want anyone using that same yardstick or pointing the same finger at us. We become negative and critical if others look at us the wrong way, but we don't want people scrutinizing how we are looking at them. This is a double standard. What we fail to realize is that if we are critical, judgmental, and unloving, it will come back to us later. It is the law of reaping and sowing, and it is as alive today as it has ever been.

5. Read Luke 6:41-42.

∞ What does this passage mean to you?

∞ Do you have trouble with pointing the finger or placing blame on others? Why do you think you struggle with this?

∞ Have you ever looked inside yourself, asking God to show you your own heart?

> *When you are pointing your finger at someone, you have three of your own fingers pointing back at you! Try it, you'll see.*

It is amazing how we can quote verses such as Luke 6:41-42, but we do not live them. Mercy has not become a habitual part of our relationships. A merciful person is kind and compassionate and eager to forgive!

6. Write out Hosea 6:6.

∞ Write out Matthew 9:12-13.

We can serve in church ministries until the Lord comes back and still not live as merciful people. One of the worst places for unkindness is right within the local church. This is a sad statement of truth! We sacrifice our time, our money, and our lifestyles when in front of people, but what God really desires is that we love people. He desires mercy and not our sacrificial service that is laced with gossip, judgmental attitudes, and finger pointing. He desires that we walk in His love. That love hopes for the best in all people—the opposite of gazing at others with a critical eye. How do you treat others? Honestly. Remember, kind and compassionate treatment is a sign of a merciful heart.

7. **Read Matthew 23:23-28.**

∞ This is a very strong passage of Scripture, and these are the words of Christ. What three things did Jesus tell the Pharisees they had neglected? (v. 23)

• 1.

• 2.

• 3.

∞ What word does Jesus use to describe the Pharisees when they neglected these things?

8. **What do you think of the cup and dish analogy in Matthew 23:25-26?**

∞ Have you been guilty of being concerned only with appearances? Explain.

Justice:
fairness

Mercy:
kindness

Faithfulness:
*consistency with the facts,
steadfast in nature*

∞ Based on these verses, how do you suppose you obtain mercy to give to others?

9. **Write out Lamentations 3:22-23.**

It is because of His mercy that we are not consumed. And each day we receive a new shipment of God's mercy and love. Do you suppose that he can show you what it means to live in new mercies each day?

Some people have the mistaken idea that mercy is just the gift of caring and running around doing things for others. While doing these things is indeed kind and compassionate, it is not the essence of mercy. Mercy is an attitude of the heart. It is something that flows from the inside out. All believers can have mercy if they ask God for an internal overhaul. Mercy is part of the nature of God, and therefore it is part of what He is making us to be.

10. **Read James 4:1-4.**

The battle is within us, and that is why the inside of the cup must be cleaned. If the inside heart is clean, and the attitude in check, then the outside will sparkle with the beauty of mercy. But, just as with anything else, we won't have mercy if we don't ask for it. Mercy is one of God's riches, and we can and should ask the Father to give us this wonderful attribute because with mercy we can truly love others with the love of the Father.

∞ Write out the following verses.
  • Proverbs 11:17:

  • Micah 6:8:

  • Matthew 5:7:

11. Read James 3:13-18.

∞ List the components of earthly wisdom.

∞ List the components of heavenly wisdom.

∞ Of what is heavenly wisdom full?

12. Read Matthew 5:1-9.

Mercy is a lot like forgiveness. If we show mercy, we too will receive mercy. You may not receive it today, but God's Word is true, and you will receive from Him what you have sown in other's lives. I think it is interesting that Jesus says peacemakers will be blessed and be called His children. He doesn't say the argumentative will be blessed. No. They are just doing battle and will pay for it in the end, either through circumstances or health issues. Being unkind, unforgiving, and unmerciful causes much stress to the mind and body. It is more work than it is worth, but it is what comes naturally to most of us when we are crossed. Once we get it in our heads that God desires us to be merciful people and that He will provide the mercy we need, we can move forward by faith.

As my mother advanced in age, she needed help and care. She came to live with us in our downstairs bedroom. Many times I was frustrated with her. She had so many needs, and she seemed to be so demanding and negative. After a few years of this, I was becoming tired of taking care of her. It was then that I asked God to give me His heart of mercy toward my mother. The next day as I took her breakfast, I looked at her with different eyes. I gradually began to see some of the reasons she had fallen into the negative—her life had become painful and hard, and she didn't know how to grow old peacefully. I began to realize the frustration she felt because she had to be cared for as her health failed her.

> *I will give them singleness of heart and put a new spirit within them. I will take away their hearts of stone and give them tender hearts instead* (Ezekiel 11:19, NLT).

Seeing her through different eyes began to change the way I treated her. I continued to pray for a heart of mercy for her, and the burden of her care seemed to lift from my heart. I realized I had an opportunity to be a channel of God's love to someone who was shut indoors and desperately needed cheer. As my attitude became more merciful, her attitude also changed. It was then that I realized being merciful to her was a good thing for me too (Proverbs 11:17).

Surely goodness and mercy will follow me all the days of my life (Psalm 23:6, KJV).

∽ List some ways that you can show mercy to the people God has placed in your life.

From the Heart

Mend a quarrel.
Search out a forgotten friend.
Dismiss a suspicion and replace it with a trust.
Write a letter to someone who misses you.
Encourage a youth who has lost his faith.
Keep a promise.
Forget an old grudge.
Examine your demands on others.
Fight for a principle.
Express your gratitude.
Overcome an old fear.
Take time to appreciate the beauty of nature.
Give God the praise.
Tell them again, and again, and again.
—*Author unknown*

A tender heart is a heart of mercy. Ask God for a new heart today. Ask Him by the power of His Spirit to fill you with His wonderful mercy.

Father,

I am limited within myself when it comes to mercy. But I come asking You to fill me with a merciful attitude toward the people You have placed in my life. May I learn to treat others with dignity and love. Give me a tender heart, one that looks beyond the natural and into the spirit of a person. I do want to walk in Your love and Your mercy. Teach me how to do this, show me the way. Amen.

LIVING KINDNESS . . . THE REFRESHED LIFE

"A generous man will prosper; he who refreshes others will himself be refreshed" (Proverbs 11:25).

Kindness can be very practical and it can be very spiritual. In this lesson we will look at both sides of kindness.

1. **Write out Ephesians 4:32.**

We have looked at this verse several times in this study. That's okay because repetition gives way to permanency in our hearts and minds, and this results in a conviction that produces lifestyle change. This verse tells us there are three things that should characterize our relationships:

> kindness
> compassion
> forgiveness

Kind: warm-hearted, friendly, generous with good will, pleasant, agreeable, accommodating.

Jesus Christ is all of these things in His relationship with us. He is the model of what a relationship should look like. We are imperfect people and we have funny sin-based ideas of how we should treat people. Everything in our lives does not change overnight when we become Christians, but our spirit changes, that which we cannot see, promising us eternal life. Our natural man begins to change as we draw near to God, seek His ways, learn what His will is, and follow after Him.

This explains why some Christians are mean, cranky, and not at all exemplifying those three attributes of kindness, compassion, and forgiveness. Why? Because perhaps they have not been told about the lifestyle in which you remain connected to Christ, receiving the flow of His love, His spirit, and His wisdom into your practical life day by day. And, perhaps they did not realize that they were to take God's Word seriously in the practical applications of how to live out their lives.

Does this describe you?

When we do take God's Word as serious guidance material, our lives change, our spirits soar, and we are lifted up out of the gunk that we have been accustomed to dwelling in.

We have all grown up with patterns of how to treat people. Perhaps you did not like the way your parents or siblings acted, and you feel that your actions now are much better than those of your family of origin. But, are you looking to Jesus for the pattern of how to treat others? Don't look to the pattern of other people, look into the Word of Truth and find the pattern that will please God and bring freedom to your heart and relationships.

1 Corinthians 13 says that love is kind. Kindness is definitely something that we should pay attention to and pursue because kindness is love, and God tells us we are to pursue and follow after love. This may be uncomfortable for you. In fact, this may be extremely uncomfortable for you. That's okay. God's Word is often uncomfortable for us to follow. We usually are living contrary to His Word because we haven't learned what it means to walk in the Spirit. When we walk in the Spirit we do not fulfill the ugly stuff of the flesh. Kindness is walking in the Spirit.

2. Write out Ephesians 5:1-2.

⊙ According to these verses, whom are you to imitate?

∞ What describes God's attitude toward you?

∞ How are you then to live?

> People who live long lives together eventually begin to sound
> alike, to talk alike, even to think alike. As we walk with God,
> we take on His thoughts, His principles, His attitudes. We
> take on His heart.[1] —*Max Lucado*

To imitate means to mimic. We are to mimic or copy the patterns of
Jesus. But, God's Word never directs us to rely on our own power for effec-
tive change. We are to obey God, follow after His pattern, and pray for God
to do the work of Christ deep within us. I have heard it said that this is like
praying toward heaven and rowing toward shore! We actively seek to walk
in His ways and obey His precepts, but we are first actively praying for God
to do His work in us.

3. Write out Ephesians 5:8-10.

See the difference here? The Bible says that you were dark and now you
are light. Far too often we live in the dark in our dealings with others. We
are to find out *what pleases the Lord,* and remain there.

4. Write out Ephesians 5:15.

∞ What does this verse tell you about how you should live?

∞ Read James 1:5.
∞ How do you become wise?

5. **Read James 3:13-18.**
∞ If you are receiving wisdom from God, how will your actions change?

∞ Will you think you are superior spiritually?

∞ Are envy and selfishness spiritual?

∞ What will be present when there is bitter envy and selfish ambition in your life?

∞ What characteristics will you begin to take on when you are walking in the wisdom and will of God?

∞ Do you like the idea of being a peacemaker? Why or why not?

Right about now, you might be thinking, *but what about the difficult people in my life?* Good point! Let's see what God says about dealing with the difficult people and the difficult circumstances in our lives.

When People Do Not Accept You

6. Read Matthew 10:11-14.

Jesus was giving His disciples instruction for their ministry trip. He knew some people would not accept them or help them in any way.

∞ What did Jesus tell the disciple to do when they were not welcomed?

Notice that He did not tell the disciples to defend themselves, explain themselves, argue their point, or spend days in endless discussions about why they should be welcomed. No. Jesus instructed the disciples simply to go on their way with no worry about the people who did not want to have anything to do with them. The disciples were to shake the dust off their feet and leave those people to God without the arguments and hard feelings that are so prevalent in relationships and churches today.

∞ What does the saying "I agree to disagree" mean to you?

7. Continue reading in Matthew 10:17-20.

In this passage Jesus gives the disciples instruction for their pending persecution. Though most of us will not experience flogging or this type of persecution, there is an important attitude here that we can apply to our situations.

Do not worry.

The Spirit will speak through you.

In this life we will be faced with a different kind of trauma in our relationships. Our relationships are plagued with selfishness. We will have to walk into situations where we will not know what to say. We will not know what key will unlock the misunderstanding. That is why it is so important to stay close, connected, in tune, grafted in, surrendered, sold out, submitted to the Father.

As we walk in the Spirit, we will be in tune with the Spirit, and that same Spirit will speak through us according to the wisdom of God, which, by the way, is peaceable!

8. **Read Galatians 5:16-26.**

∽ What is in conflict within you? (vv. 16-17)

∽ What are the characteristics of human flesh that damage relationships? (vv. 19-21)

∽ What are the characteristics of the Spirit that give new life to relationships? (vv. 22-23)

∽ Whom are you to keep in step with? (v. 25)

∽ What are you not to do to others? (v. 26)

∽ If you were to take just this passage seriously, how would it change any of your current dealings with people?

What If There Is a Problem?

9. **Read Matthew 18:15-17.**

∽ What are you to do if someone sins against you?

∽ Whom is the conversation to be between?

∽ What if the person does not listen to you?

Too many times, especially as women, we go around the block several times with a problem before taking it to the person involved. This is gossip and talebearing. Ouch!

When you have a problem, as uncomfortable as it might seem, take it directly to the source, and follow the way of the Word:

speak the truth in love,

have kindness on your tongue.

10. **Let's look more closely at the things that may come naturally to us but damage our relationships: hatred, anger, resentment, and bitterness.**

Hatred: animosity and hostility

Hatred doesn't happen overnight. It is what happens when you aren't dealing correctly with a problem when it first hits the scene, or when your pent-up stuff hits the fan! You've been wronged; you became angry. What did you do with that anger? Did you allow it to fester into true hostility? Not a pretty sight, is it?

Anger: a strong feeling of displeasure, becoming mad or irate

Anger is a normal human emotion. Not everything in your life will please you, and not every person in your path will either. You will never be completely free of this emotion in this life. Things will happen to make you angry. There is nothing wrong with the feeling of anger—it is what we do with anger that counts.

Let's look at God's way of handling anger.

Anger Conceived

" . . . a harsh word stirs up anger" (Proverbs 15:1).

Ever notice how a harsh word seems to stir up your defense mechanisms? Someone has wronged you, and everything within you wants to scream at that person or at someone else who is available! At the moment the matchstick of anger was lit, you could choose to fight back and fan the flame, or you could trust God with the circumstance and handle the conflict in a healthy way. The beginning of the Proverbs 15:1 verse states: "A gentle answer turns away wrath . . ."

The Face of Anger

Often we rage when someone has wronged us. We give full vent because, we justify, this person deserves a piece of my mind, and he or she will not walk on me! According to Scripture this is how a fool deals with anger.

In contrast, when we are filled with God's wisdom, we will keep the anger in control. We will not deny the anger or the problem that caused it, but instead we will:

A fool gives full vent to his anger, but a wise man keeps himself under control (Proverbs 29:11).

- speak the truth in love (Ephesians 4:15);
- deal with the problem humbly (Ephesians 4:2).

Remember to allow God to work. Everything doesn't have to be solved today

Diverting Resentment and Bitterness, By-products of Anger

11. Write out Psalm 4:4-5.

You will not become a bitter person if you deal with a problem and then close the book on it, only opening the book if the problem arises again, then dealing with it once again and moving on. In Psalm 4:4-5 we see the picture of someone going away alone to bed and dealing with anger by offering a right sacrifice to God—surrendering the heart to God's will. When we follow the psalmist's example, God can minister to us and help us deal with any mistreatment. Instead of calling on every friend, try calling on Almighty God!

If you do not choose to move on, you give the Devil a foothold in your life.

A foothold means: a position providing a place for advancement.

12. Write out Ephesians 4:26-27.

You should memorize this verse. I can not tell you how the application of it is helping me. I recognize that I will have anger from time to time. That's normal, I've accepted that. But, now I keep myself on a time clock, literally. It seems to me that my anger should not spill over into another day. Or, to break it down practically, once twenty-four hours have passed, I better move on! Sometimes I let myself stew a few hours, but because I know it is not good to hold on to these things, I work at giving it to God and moving on. If the angry thoughts come back to haunt me, guess what? I take them back to the Lord and humble myself before Him. Regardless of my feelings at this point I am to act appropriately, according to the Spirit, even if the other person is not. This is where kindness comes in!

13. Read James 1:19-25.

∽ Why do you suppose James writes, "Take note of this"? (v. 19)

∽ What three things does James urge you to do in verse 19?
  1.
  2.
  3.

14. Jealousy also negatively impacts relationships. Write out Galatians 6:4.

You are not to compare yourself with another person. You should write that one hundred times, like a child who hasn't learned a fine point in school . . . just kidding, but it wouldn't hurt. Women are so prone to competition and comparisons, and that leads to jealousy or pride. Either one wrecks relationships and robs people of the ability to be kind. Jealously is simply envy over something someone else has that *you think* you don't have. The emphasis is on *think* because you are really okay and have just what you need, but you think you don't; therefore, you compare, complain, feel insecure, and get jealous. Being jealous is one of the works of the flesh.

15. Read 1 Corinthians 3:3-9.

∞ Write out 1 Corinthians 3:3.

We do not need to be jealous because God has a purpose for each person. Let's get a grip here! If I am not gifted in areas that you are, then I must accept that our gifts were assigned us by the will of God. Again, what we really need is more connection to Jesus, more faith, and more perspective on the big picture and His love for us as individuals. His love is kind, and we can learn to be kind to one another when we realize that no one is a threat to us because God will accomplish all He has planned for our life.

16. Let's look at what our relationships will have in them when we are in step with the Spirit. Open up again to Galatians 5:22. Let's concentrate on part of the fruit of the Spirit—kindness.

> *Kindness: pleasant, courteous, respecting others, honoring others, and blessing them*

∞ Read Colossians 3:12-17.
∞ According to this passage, what are you to put on like clothing?

∞ Do you think this applies to everyone in your life, or just to the people you like? Elaborate.

∞ Read James 2:1-9.
This passage speaks to giving more honor to the rich, but it makes the point clear that God has no favorites. We should not apply His words and teachings only to our friends or to our convenient people. We are to apply His Word to all people we come in contact with.

You will be surprised at what will happen when you begin to act kindly to those who have hurt you or wronged you. Act kindly just because it pleases the Father. Do it according to the will of God and the Word of God and watch as you are filled with the fruits of righteousness yourself. Peace will be yours and so will forgiveness and mercy. It will feel strange at first. But, it is God's way.

17. Read Hebrews 12:14-15 and Hebrews 13:1.

∞ Journal your thoughts here regarding this lesson on kindness and what God is speaking to you.

∞ List some practical ways you can show kindness to someone today.

Here are some of the practical things on my list:
    smile
    hold my tongue
    speak pleasantly
    listen
    ask questions about the person's life
    bake cookies
    send a card
    buy a gift
    say a prayer
    give a hug

do someone else's chore
be helpful
smile again
do not judge the person
accept your differences
do not compete with another person
give the other person space
find out what this person really needs and provide it (a night out, a car
  wash . . .)
pick up the phone and say hello
send flowers
extend respect and courtesy even to someone who dislikes me

Choosing not to sweat the small stuff, accepting another warts and all—
that is kindness. Remember: "Love is a God-given opportunity to refresh
and encourage another." Be on the lookout for those God-given opportunities!

Father,

*Many times I am just not kind at all. I want my own way, am grumpy,
moody, or irritable, and I just don't feel like being kind. After all, many people aren't kind to me either. But, I realize that You have something better
for me than living in the immaturity of my childish ways. I am just a child
when I withhold kindness from another person. Today, may I smile more,
and may I be more aware of what it means to be kind. Give me the grace
to deal with anger as it comes up and teach me Your way of handling conflict. Amen.*

*L*IVING REAL . . .
THE PRACTICAL SIDE OF LOVE

Love is proven by actions.

Practically speaking, love isn't love if it is in theory only. We can talk about love and its attributes, but if love is not in our lives at the down to earth, rubber-meets-the-road level, then we are just all talk. This is exactly what non-Christians complain about the most when asked about Christians. They think we are all talk and hot-air hypocrites.

This is an unfortunate judgment because even non-Christians do not practice everything they preach. The best thing I ever heard said about our actions is: preach Christ always, use words as little as possible.

We are to live the love of God, not just talk about it. We seem to know a lot in our heads, but we do not see the evidence of the things we know practiced on the daily, real-life level. When you meet Christians who are practicing what they believe to be God's way, it is refreshing and exciting. It gives us hope that the spirit of Christ can become a part of our lives on a practical level.

Practical: *serving a purpose, useful, practice, use rather than theory or speculation, sensible, functional, handy.*

Well . . . guess what? Jesus wants to be very much a part of your life on a practical level too. He wants to make you a vessel of His awesome and magnificent love, poured out to everyone you come in contact with. Does this mean you are sickeningly sweet? No, no, no. It means you are to be passionately surrendered to the outpouring of His

Spirit. He will make His work in you very, very practical.

1. Read James 2:14-17.
∞ What is this passage saying to you?

2. Read Matthew 25:31-40
∞ Do you see the practical side of love here? Explain.

∞ What are the action parts in this passage?

It is obvious that Jesus was teaching those who were listening that everything they do, they do for Him. Not just acts of worship, church services, or evangelical ministries, but even the everyday practical things. Feeding someone, meeting a need for someone, visiting someone who needs a visitor . . . all these things are very down-to-earth practical things. And each of these things represent the practical side of our spirituality. These things are the deeds and the works that must accompany our faith in order for us to live out our faith in this world we live in.

3. Read on in Matthew 25:41-45.
∞ This is the picture of faith with no works. What is this saying to you?

4. **Read 2 Timothy 2:20-25.**

Vessel: a hollow utensil used as a container.

In my office I have a few things that are meaningful to me. At first glance some might wonder why I have certain little props in my sitting area. Above the small table that is surrounded with two chairs, there hangs a beautiful picture. But, it is not just any picture. At first glance it looks like a lovely Thomas Kinkade, but when you look closer, you see it's a Kinkade puzzle, with all the intricate pieces neatly glued into one beautiful work of art. This is my reminder of Romans 8:28.

On the table under the picture there is a very small wrapped gift. The gift reminds me that each day is a gift and that I need to present my life daily to Jesus for His use. Finally, there is a small miniature metal pitcher. A simple metal pitcher, empty and with no decorative touch. It is unbreakable and unbendable. This reminds me that God desires to pour through my life as His vessel, His little pitcher. I need to remain the empty vessel through which He may pour His love, His grace, His kindness, and His mercy to others.

Sometimes I just look inside the empty little pitcher and remind myself that Jesus wants me emptied of self so that I will not touch or taint the work of His Spirit.

∞ Jesus has called each of us to be an instrument of noble purposes. According to 2 Timothy 2:20-25, what are the things He says He will do in you?

He will make me:
1.
2.
3.

5. **Verse 22 says you are to:**
   flee evil desires
   pursue righteousness
   pursue faith
   pursue love
   pursue peace

To pursue righteousness means you are seeking to please God, and you are pursuing anything and everything that will make your walk pleasing to God. Part of pursuing faith, love, and peace involves keeping track of our tongues.

∞ According to verses 23-25, what should you not do?

6. One practical way to show others the love of God is to speak kindly of them. Look up the following verses and write out the one that is most meaningful to you. Then commit it to memory this week.
   • Proverbs 11:13:

   • Proverbs 16:28:

   • Proverbs 26:20:

   • 1 Corinthians 13:7:

   • Galatians 5:14-15:

   • James 1:26:

   • James 3:9:

   • James 5:9:

7. **Write your thoughts about the verse you just chose to memorize.**

8. **Read Hebrews 11.**

∞ According to this chapter, what practical things did the men and women of old do?

∞ How did they live?

9. **Write out Hebrews 10:38.**

Imagine your name in this verse. I can read it this way: "Debbie will live by faith, and if she shrinks back from that faith, God will not be pleased with her."

I want God to be pleased with me—that is my life's goal. I desire to know Him more and more, and to live a life pleasing to Him. When I do certain actions by faith, that pleases God. When I shrink back because of my own fear or my own flesh, He is not pleased with my choice to do so.

Remember that sometimes you have to act out love and part of that is doing those things that are scriptural for you to do. Don't wait to *feel* anything. That isn't faith! Anyone can love and do practical acts of kindness and love without feeling warm and fuzzy toward someone. But, it is when you feel dead and empty, yet you still walk in love according to God's Word, that you please Him. It is then that God's love can break through you.

10. **Write out Hebrews 13:15-16.**

∞ Through whom are you to live and love?

∞ What are you not to forget?

∞ What do you think the word *sacrifice* means here?

Doing good to others is somewhat of a sacrifice isn't it? You have to forfeit your own feelings
sometimes, giving those feelings to God and
believing by faith that He will cause you to love
other people His way. It is also a sacrifice for us
when we are tired, sick, busy, or emotionally spent

> **Sacrifice:**
> *forfeiture of some-*
> *thing valuable for*
> *the sake of some-*
> *thing else.*

ourselves. Some women suffer great hormonal
swings, and any act of kindness they make might be through gritted teeth.
Nevertheless, we are to offer God this sacrifice, obeying His will and living
His Word out in practical ways.

11. Take a personal inventory of the people in your life with whom you
    have unfinished business. You cannot change other people, but you
    can submit yourself to God. After each name, jot down ideas of
    things you can do for these people that would be a practical way of
    you living out your faith despite their lack of cooperation.

> *But you are a chosen people, a royal priesthood, a holy nation, a people belonging to God, that you may declare the praises of him who called you out of darkness into his wonderful light (1 Peter 2:9).*

Let us live in the light of love by faith! Each day everything we do has an impact. Let's make it our goal to leave the heartprint of Jesus on everything and everyone we touch today. Remember, we are only responsible for our actions, not another's response. Let the Spirit fill you and flow through you to others as you live in kindness and love as His everyday vessel. Loving God and loving others is real and practical—let's live in the practical side of love.

HeartPrints

Whatever our hands touch—
We leave fingerprints!
On walls, on furniture,
On doorknobs, dishes, books.
There's no escape.
As we touch we leave our identity.

O God, wherever I go today
Help me to leave heartprints!
Heartprints of compassion
Of understanding and love.
Heartprints of kindness
And genuine concern.
May my heart touch a lonely neighbor
Or a runaway daughter
Or an anxious mother
Or perhaps an aged grandfather.

Lord, send me out today
To leave heartprints.
And if someone should say,
"I felt your touch,"
May that one sense Your love
Touching through me.[1]
—*Ruth Harm Calkins*

Father,

I desire to leave Your heartprints everywhere I go. May my life be an encouraging word to a discouraged person. May I be open to Your leading as You shape me into a vessel for Your use. I ask You to use me today and every-day, according to Your power that is at work within me . . . the power of love. Amen.

LIVING UNSELFISHLY . . . SEEKING ANOTHER'S BEST

". . . building others up according to their needs"
(Ephesians 4:29).

Love is not a feeling. It is an overwhelming passion to help and bless and deliver and comfort and strengthen and give joy to others just as the Lord Jesus always did.

Living to seek another's best is living as God's everyday vessel. Often we try and do what's best for someone else, but end up feeling frustrated because we have been unsuccessful at meeting the need of another person. It is important that we recognize we must first seek God before we can seek to be a blessing of God to another person. If we are not seeking God and are not in fellowship with Him, we will not deliver the very things only God's Spirit knows another person needs. We will be delivering our own goodwill, but that goodwill runs short and empties out over time. Our own goodwill gets frustrated when unrecognized, and then the whole vicious cycle of relational problems begins again.

When we are operating out of God's resource of love, we trust that He is using us as His vessel. He will give us the wisdom and grace to display just the right touch that the receiver needs at the time. When we are not recognized for the good deeds, we will dismiss it, knowing that we are asking God to love through us, and the outcome is His business. In other words, when we do things God's way, seeking first His kingdom, we will have peace and all the things we need will be added to us as we serve Him.

Let's look at some relational roles we may fall into.

The Employee

1. **Read Ephesians 6:5-8, writing out verse 6.**

It is hard to see the word *slave* and relate to it. But it just refers to any-one who is working for another. According to this passage, there are certain things that are appropriate for us to have toward our employer. They are:

respect,

fear, the reverence of fear,

sincere hearts toward the employer,

obedience to the rules of our employer.

Many people work in environments where the only thing that they have is the obedience to the rules. They do not respect, honor, or have sincere hearts toward the one who is providing a job for them. And, to fuel this, there may be good reason for these difficulties. Now here comes the choice. As a Christian, you are to follow the example of Christ, who always put another first, knowing that God the Father would take care of Him. He was obedient to the death on the cross; therefore, even in the event that you do not agree with everything about your employer as a person, Scripture clearly outlines some things for you to do. They are:

obey and respect your employer,

serve wholeheartedly,

We must remember who we are really obeying and serving.

∞ Whose employee are you during that work shift? Why?

∞ What will the Lord do when you make this choice?

By giving your best work, you are seeking the best for your employer and also for the company. You are also lining yourself up with scriptural and spiritual principles.

2. Write out 1 Peter 2:18-19.

∞ Are you to respect even those who do not deserve it? Why?

The key element here is *being conscious of God.* There is that seeking God concept again! The Bible is really so basic for our living needs. We just somehow keep overlooking the basics. Why do you think we do that? Do you suppose these truths are so simplistic that they seem impractical and therefore hard to follow? Journal your thoughts here.

The Employer or Supervisor

3. Write out Ephesians 6:9.

Wow! Is this ever important to remember for those who are in authority over others. There is no favoritism with God. He loves all people the same, and there are not different levels of people, just people that He created. Some people have a position of higher authority in this life, but that does not mean anything to God except that those people are to treat those under them with respect and serve them with a sincere heart, seeking their best.

This is a concept that has many rewards. If the employer or overseer is good to his or her people, then they will naturally want to please the employer by giving their best effort. As Christians, we need to be convinced that our best is always what we are called to give regardless of circumstances. In every situation the employer who looks out for the good of his or her employees will be rewarded with respect and hard work.

The Workplace

4. **Read 1 Peter 2:9-17.**

∞ Write out verse 17.

"But I can't," you say. "I just can't live this good life!"

No kidding. Neither can I in my strength or power, and neither could the Apostle Paul. Always doing the right thing goes against my ego and my natural tendencies. I am comforted that it's not just me, but everyone who struggles with this. Even the most spiritual-looking person (How do you look spiritual? I never have figured that out!) or the most pious-acting person struggles with SELF. Take Paul's word for it in the book of Romans.

5. **Read Romans 7:14–8:14.**

∞ Do you ever relate with Paul—knowing the things you should not do, yet doing them anyway? Give an example that relates to your relationship with another person.

Friends, this world is not your home, so don't make your-selves cozy in it. Don't indulge your ego at the expense of your soul. Live an exemplary life among the natives so that your actions will refute their prejudices. Then they'll be won over to God's side and be there to join in the celebration when he arrives (1 Peter 2:11–12, TM).

∞ Write out Romans 7:18.

> I know that all God's commands are spiritual, but I'm not. Isn't this also your experience? Yes. I am full of myself—after all, I've spent a long time in sin's prison. What I don't understand about myself is that I decide one way, but then act in another, doing things I absolutely despise. So if I can't be trusted to figure out what is best for myself and then do it, it becomes obvious that God's command is necessary (Romans 7:14-16, TM).

6. What do you think it means to be led by the Spirit of God?

∞ Do you want to be led by the Spirit of God in your relationships? Why?

1 Corinthians 13:5 says that love is not self-seeking. If we are led by the Spirit of God into God's love, we will have relationships that are characterized by seeking another person's BEST.

∞ Write out 1 Corinthians 10:23.

∞ Write out Philippians 2:4.

7. Read Philippians 2:13-21.

I find it encouraging that it is God who works in me, to change my will to bring it in line with His! Philippians 2:13 has been my marinade over the past six months. What I mean by that is that I have been soaking in this verse for many months now. When I soak in a verse, it begins to sink into my thick skin and become part of the flavor of who I am. I have noticed that now when I am discouraged, I am more apt to remind myself that God is working in me to will and to do His good pleasure for my life. And, when there is noticeable fruit (a miracle!) I can be excited that it is God working in me, bringing me in line with His plan and His design for me individually so that *He may be glorified.*

∞ We are to do everything without what? (See Philippians 2:14.)

∞ What do most people do? (v. 21)

∞ Do you think it is scriptural to look out for others? Explain.

We live in a "Me First," "Take Care of #1" society. Because of this, it is hard to take the Word of God seriously, but we must purpose in our hearts not only to be a loving people, but also to be a people who are unselfish and caring for others.

Now let's move from workplace to home.

The Home

8. **Read Ephesians 5:21-24, 32-33.**

Submit? Is that a hard, ugly word to you? Did you know that one of the definitions of submit is *to be in consideration of someone else?* When picturing *submit* in today's terms, I see a used and abused wife, struggling for some individuality and identity, a servant to her husband's whims, desires, and commands. But, actually this is not the scriptural focus of submission at all. Remember, God always works in our lives out of His love for us. He, therefore, always gives us directives that will be good for us and not harm us. We do not have to be afraid of God's will, nor do we have to be selective about what we will obey in His Word. If it is in His Word, it is always for our best. (Look at it this way: Jesus seeks our best all the time, and now we are learning that trait of seeking another's best.)

∞ Write out Ephesians 5:21.

Notice this verse says we are to submit to one another. This isn't just speaking about marriage—this is to be the norm in all relationships. Read Ephesians 5:15-21, and you can see this is talking about all human relations. We are to respect one another, being considerate of one another because we love God and want to please Him.

9. **Write out Ephesians 5:32-33.**

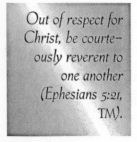

Out of respect for Christ, be courteously reverent to one another (Ephesians 5:21, TM).

The profound mystery is how God can take two lives and join them spiritually as one. And, this does not just describe marriage but also the mystery of our relationship with Jesus Christ. We are born into this world as flesh and are reborn by the Spirit of Christ, making us one with Him. This is a mystery. And just as Christ loves us, and we respect God and His ways, husbands are to love their wives, and wives are to respect their husbands. But . . . what about the mean ones? What if my husband doesn't love me, or the Lord, or anything other than himself? It is then we must go back to Ephesians 5:21.

Being courteous to your mate doesn't mean you always have to agree. It doesn't mean you cannot give your opinion. It also doesn't mean that you should put up with actual abuse of any form. If you feel you are in an abusive situation, you should seek professional help. By the way, living with a husband who is less than perfect does not constitute abuse. If you are in actual abuse, you probably know it without anyone telling you. Remember, speaking up and getting help in an abusive situation could be seeking another's best. Sometimes people don't change because they aren't required to.

"We always hurt the ones we love," is an old saying that rings with truth. That is why we need to learn to walk in the Spirit and ask God by His power to teach us the walk of love with our mates. Seeking their best may be agreeing to that fishing trip or football game. Husbands need space too, and they need your love and support. Sometimes we get so bogged down with our responsibilities that we feel overwhelmed and forget that husbands get overwhelmed too. When was the last time you looked at your husband and actually tried on his shoes, to see how you could best support him?

> *Wives, understand and support your husbands in ways that show your support for Christ (Ephesians 5:22, TM).*

Relationships with Your Children

10. Read Colossians 3:21.

∞ What happens when you are too hard on your children?

∞ Read Proverbs 31:27-28.

This passage shows us a picture of a woman who is living to seek the best for her family, and in the end they call her blessed and praise her for all her love and attention.

You will teach your children *about* love *by* loving. Children learn more from our actions than our words. If I tell my children God is love, and they see me not loving, than they will get a mixed message. The powerful legacy that God has given us to pass to our children is Jesus Christ and His love. We must be a loving people if this is going to have this impact. Remember, your choice today makes a ripple effect tomorrow.

Relationships with Your Parents

11. Read Ephesians 6:2-3.

As adults we still have a responsibility to our parents. We are to honor them. This means we are to esteem, respect, and treat them kindly. And, like all other relationships, we are to seek their best.

∞ Ephesians 6:3 actually contains a promise. What is that promise?

For some of you this concept of honoring your parents is very hard to swallow. Your parents may be mean and, certainly in your mind, undeserving of your honor. But what does Scripture say? What would Jesus do? What are you to do?

Give your attitude about your parents to Christ.

Pray for your parents.

Ask God by His Spirit to work in you His love for your parents.

By faith, act respectfully, even before the feelings come.

Walk in kindness and honor as to the Lord.

Sometimes honoring your parents will mean honoring their wishes. For me, that has been a challenge at times. Both my sister and I wanted to honor our mom's wishes to stay out of a nursing home. We set our hearts to do whatever we had to do to take care of a sick, elderly parent. It wasn't easy. Sometimes we just had to do what was right by faith alone. And, always we had to pray and ask God to love her and take care of her through us.

We are imperfect daughters, He is a perfect God, so we want to take on His characteristics. This was our prayer while our mother was alive. I know I can speak for my sister in saying that we both now see that the time with our mother was a gift to us. It changed us, it stretched us, it caused us to grow. But, most of all, it gave us a different love for our mother and healed up any old wounds. We have no regrets. In taking care of her, we have been blessed.

Do you have aging parents? Do you look for ways to honor them and seek their best interest? A visit would be nice, so would cards, regular phone calls, and especially regular prayer. How do you wish to be treated when you are old? Think about it, and treat your parents with the same tenderness, kindness, and respect. Out of steam and fuel for love? Ask Jesus!

Relationships with Your EGR People
(Extra Grace Required)

Usually these relationships are ones that you did not choose: a relative, ex-relative, in-law, ex-law, coworker, or neighbor. Perhaps you did not choose a relationship with this person, but nevertheless he or she is now in your life and because of that, you are responsible for how you choose to treat him or her.

These relationships are the most challenging because sometimes these people are difficult or hard to warm up to. They can be judgmental, argumentative, and offer you all sorts of unfair and undeserved treatment.

12. Read 1 Thessalonians 4:1-11.
With what kind of instruction does this chapter begin?

Beginning with verse 9, what is being spoken about?

What are the key points of verses 11-12?
- Lead a

- Mind your

- Work with

- So that

- You will not

With the difficult people in our lives, it is important that we concentrate on our own accountability with the Lord. We need to be certain that we are living a life that pleases God. We must honor others with respectful and courteous behavior no matter how they treat us. The only way to do this is to fix our eyes on Jesus and depend solely on the Lord and His Spirit.

13. Read 1 Thessalonians 5:14-24.
This passage is encouraging you to seek another's best through the love

of God. It actually says, "*make sure* that nobody pays back wrong for wrong, but always try to be kind to each other and to everyone else" (v. 15).

∞ Do you think this includes your EGR people? Journal your thoughts on this or write about a particular instance that comes to mind.

We certainly live in a complex society. The family unit is not in one neat little package anymore. It was hard to live peacefully within the parameters of a traditional family unit. But, now with the divorce rate in the 70 percentile, we are a country filled with families that are all mixed up, bruised, broken, and we call this the "blended family."

Many of you as Christians are in a blended family unit, or are single mothers dealing with the remnant of divorce. Though this study is not on divorce, there is something worthy of comment here. You must include all the EGR people that are in your life in the mix of obeying Scripture. Your ex-husband is not excluded from God's command for you to love, and neither are any of your new blended family members.

I speak to Christian women frequently who refuse to have anything to do with their ex-spouses. This gives a double message to your children. Live to seek another's best, your children's best, and their children's best, by choosing to live at peace. You do not have to hang out or be close friends with your ex-spouse—that portion of life is gone. But, you do owe that person courteous respect and forgiveness. Remember the Lord and your children. Keep in mind the legacy you want to leave!

For many years I coordinated weddings for a local church. In this position I came across many families who were going through a big life event without the original family intact. It never ceased to amaze me how the Christians in these situations often acted. Glaring at each other, not speaking to each other, sniping each other with words and passing messages through me . . . the wedding coordinator! How sad. What are we saying about our faith in these situations? Can God really give us His power and Spirit to rise above and pursue love?

14. Write out 1 Thessalonians 5:16-17.

∞ What does this verse say is God's will for you?

15. Read 1 Thessalonians 5:23-24 out loud.
∞ Write out verse 24.

Make this verse of Scripture your prayer for this week. You and I can not live to seek another's best in our own strength. Life is filled with too many bumps and hurdles for that. We need God Himself, who is the God of peace, to work in us and through us.

Father,
   We pray You will empower us to be generous with Your love that we might encourage everyone You have put in our lives, and that Your very best will be done in them, through them, and for them. Amen!

LIVING IN UNITY ... WALKING IN UNBROKEN FELLOWSHIP

"How good and pleasant it is when brothers live together in unity!" (Psalm 133:1)

Fellowship simply refers to a friendly relationship or a union of peers. But, as we have discovered, fellowship is not always so simple. With the love of Christ, fellowship and love should be our goal. Though we don't agree on everything, have different backgrounds, beliefs, and personalities, friendly relations and courteous respect should be our goal. Anyone can hate, complain, and hold bitterness. It takes a person believing in the power of a big and Almighty God to go the extra mile and take the higher road. The extra mile is crucial to fellowship. The higher road is critical to the continued flow of the love of God.

1. **Read Acts 2:42-47.**

∞ To what did the early believers devote themselves?

∞ As a result of this devotion, what took place?

∞ How did they look after each other and the good of the whole body?

∞ What was the attitude of their hearts as they met together?

∞ What work of God happened daily as a result of their devotion to each other and to God?

∞ How can this apply to the modern churches today?

2. **Read 1 John 1:1-7.**
   In order to have fellowship with each other, we must first have fellowship with the Father. This is where some Christians fall into huge traps and wonder why their church relationships are sour.

∞ According to this passage, what will stop the flow of fellowship?

∞ What is it that you need to do to have proper fellowship?

∞ What does walking in the light mean in "real terms" to you today?

3. **Read 1 John 2:7-11.**
∞ What is the quickest way to go from walking in the light to walking around blinded in the darkness?

∞ What happens when you love your brother?

∞ Why are you more stable when you walk in love?

∞ When you choose the negative impact of discord, what is the fruit of that choice?

4. Read 1 John 1:8-10.
∞ Where do you go when you know you have fallen short? Honestly.

∞ Do you really think the pity party is the place to hang out? Why or why not?

∞ If everyone sins, then why do you have such a hard time fessing up and getting on track again?

5. Write out 1 John 2:3-6.

This is powerful! We know that we are really connecting with the Father when we obey His Word. When we obey God's Word, love is made complete in us. Wow, I love that. Then comes the challenge.

∞ Write out 1 John 2:6.

WWJD? (What would Jesus do?) This seems to be a popular slogan today. It's cute, it's catchy, it has a message. Are you picking up on the message, or just using this as a catch phrase? We should always ask ourselves, "What would Jesus have me do in this circumstance, in this relationship, with my negative feelings, and so on?" Obviously, walking as Jesus did does not come naturally and does not come overnight. It also does not come without cost.

6. Read Matthew 16:24-25.
∞ What does following in Jesus' steps require?

Deny ourselves? Who are we kidding? We don't live in a society that accepts denial of our wants. We live in a society of quick fixes and instant gratification. The concept of self-denial is not widely embraced. But without it we will have a hard time living according to God's Word and living in fellowship.

7. Read James 4:1-3.
∞ What happens to destroy fellowship?

Simply put, there is no denial of selfish ambitions; therefore, our own battles within cause us to struggle with others. We want our way, we don't get it, the claws come out, and we get ugly.

8. Read James 4:7-10.
∞ What do we do then to keep ourselves free from the selfishness that destroys our fellowship with God and others?

Staying humble before the Lord is a key. Staying connected with the Father is a key. It is not an emotional state—it is a state of obedience.

9. Read James 4:11-12 and James 5:9.
Do you ever fall into the trap of slandering another person and maybe justifying your actions by covering it up with some Christian cliché, such as,

"I'm only telling you so that you can pray"?

€ What do these verses say about judging your neighbor?

€ Do you think that you can really cover up with nice padding? Explain.

€ What about grumbling? Grumbling is that under-the-breath, exasperated, "I'm trying not to say it, but it just keeps slipping out" stuff. What does James 5:9 say about this?

€ How does keeping our mouths shut encourage fellowship to grow?

Keeping our mouths shut as women is very hard, but it is something we need to set our hearts toward. We should not give ourselves the liberty to judge, grumble, or otherwise slander another person. In Christ we can do all things, and sometimes that "thing" is keeping our mouths shut!

10. Read James 3:3-12.
€ Write down what this passage is saying to you about your mouth and how you speak of others.

€ Read Proverbs 6:16-19.
€ What are the seven things the Lord hates?
   1.

   2.

   3.

4.

5.

6.

7.

God hates when we do things that promote the disunity of our fellowship. How does this apply to your situation today?

11. Read Proverbs 6:20-23.
∞ What do these verses say to you about the importance of God's Word?

12. Read Matthew 18:15-17.
∞ Think of a time when someone wronged you and broke fellowship with you. What did you do?

∞ Write in your own words the steps for restoring fellowship as given in Matthew 18:15-17.

∞ What is the end result of your fellowship with this person if there is no resolution?

This act of cutting someone off is not to be done in a hurtful or unkind manner. If you cannot find resolution, then give this person over to the Lord. Let God work. Do not try to help God by gossiping, having slanderous conversations, or trying to win people to your side. That is immature and shows you are insecure. Don't throw away your confidence in God. Trust God. You should treat this person as an acquaintance with respect and courteous kindness. This person is God's child. Remember that!

13. Read Ephesians 5:29-32.

This passage describes fellowship. Marinate in this passage. Read it over and over. Building each other up causes fellowship to grow and pleases God. Find out what the will of the Lord is, what pleases Him, then GO!

Father,

I desire to be stable in You. I don't want to let emotions rule my life and small things cloud my vision of the value in another person. I humble myself before You and ask You to mature me in my relationships with other people. And, when the fellowship is broken, I pray that I will be quick to make amends because love is what You came for. Make love a goal of my life too. Amen.

Living a New Pattern . . . The Lifestyle of Love

Love is a confident woman, one who can love because she knows she is loved by God.

We often hear about lifestyle change in the realm of diet and health concerns. A woman has a heart attack, and suddenly she is thrown into the world of fatless, saltless living. She must embark on a lifestyle change if she is going to live. No more rich and calorie-laden eating for her! Years of living in that fashion have clogged her arteries and damaged her heart's ability to function. Her life depends on this change in lifestyle.

The same is true for all of us in the spiritual sense. No more rich and flesh-expensive actions for us because years of living in the flesh have clogged our spiritual arteries and darkened our understanding of what it means to live in God's love. We suddenly may feel thrown into the world of slanderless, bitterless, and gossip-free living because the Great Physician told us that in order to live in the Spirit, we must put such ways of life behind us.

> *Lifestyle: a way of life that reflects an individual's values.*

Often our talk does not match our walk. Our way of life does not reflect our true heart-desired values. Learning to dwell in the love of God will take some attitude adjusting, exercising of self-control (part of the fruit of the Spirit), and lots of saturation in Scripture, as well as daily time in prayer. It begins with loving God with all of us . . . every bit of us. Then it moves on to understanding our value and importance as God's created being and then into honoring others because we understand that the love God has for us also extends to others.

Let's sum it all up by walking through Romans chapter 12.

1. Read Romans 12:1

co Paul here was urging believers in Rome to do something. What was it?

Offering your body is offering the whole of yourself to God. Paul tells these believers that this is what is reasonable for them to do. Prior to exhorting them to do this, he had just told them that everything came from God, and through God, and to God are all things (Romans 11:36). Now because of this they are to present themselves to God, and this is an act of WORSHIP!

Have you offered all of you to God, or do you live on an insurance policy? Are you signed up for enough coverage to just keep you from hell's flames, but not enough of Jesus to change your life and give you power to live?

Lifestyle change 1: Offer your life to God completely.

2.   Read Romans 12:2.

co   Do you feel your attitudes are in line with the world you live in? Explain.

This world has a pattern, and the pattern is contrary to God's pattern. The only way we will be in God's good and perfect will is to turn from that pattern and embrace His Word and the pattern for living found there.

co Read 2 Timothy 3:16.

co What does this verse say about God's Word?

co How can God's Word give your life a new pattern?

3. Write out Romans 12:2.

Transformed by the renewing of your mind . . . what does that mean in real terms?

Transform means to turn completely inside out, to change the condition of, and to alter the function of our hearts and minds, which are full of only "us." We are all sinful human flesh. We need God's Spirit to make us new. Our arteries have been clogged with the debris of the culture we live in. The value system of our world has been building within us for many years and it has become ours. Some of us have taken on the value system of hypocrisy, and though we've lived in church all our lives, we haven't presented our wills to God. Our arteries are clogged from attitudes that are much like the Pharisee's. We need to be changed. How does that happen?

Renewing of our minds means that when God's Word and its value system is put into our minds, we begin to think in a new and living way. We have insights we did not previously have, and we respond to all of life differently. When we are in His Word, saturated in it, marinating in it, the flavor of who we are is transformed, and we are changed!

> *Don't become so well-adjusted to your culture that you fit into it without even thinking. Instead, fix your attention on God. You'll be changed from the inside out. Readily recognize what He wants from you, and quickly respond to it. Unlike the culture around you, always dragging you down to its level of immaturity, God brings the best out of you, develops well-formed maturity in you (Romans 12:2, TM).*

4. Read Romans 12:3.

∞ What is this verse saying to you?

∞ Does this seem like a contradiction to the message that God loves you and that you are of worth and value to Him? Explain.

Lifestyle change 2: Turn away from the world's philoso- phies. Lifestyle change 3: Be changed by filling your mind with God's way.

This humbling means that you recognize that God is God and that you are not! You were created by Him and for Him, now you are to make your life subject to Him. Yes, He loves you with immeasurable love, but don't start exalting yourself because that is not God's way. God's way should lead you to an understanding of your true worth and to a desire to commit your life more fully to God as a result of that understanding.

God's way leads to confidence in your place in the world, but not to an overabundance of confidence, which would result in pride. Instead, your

Lifestyle change 4: Humble yourself before God.

confidence will be seasoned with the reality check of the fact that every good and perfect gift comes from God, so everything good within you is from God. You will desire to submit to Him more because of His marvelous love!

5. Read Romans 12:4-5.

We are all related to one body. Now this is a lifestyle change in a world where people are islands to themselves, afraid to let another person in!

Our human bodies have many parts, and each part functions differently. Yet, each part is important . . . so it is with the human race. As Christians we belong to each other.

> In this way we are like the various parts of a human body. Each part gets its meaning from the body as a whole, not the other way around. The body we are talking about is Christ's body of chosen people. Each of us finds our meaning and function as part of his body. But as a chopped-off finger or cut-off toe we wouldn't amount to much, would we? So since we find our-selves fashioned into all these excellently formed and mar-velously functioning parts in Christ's body, let's just go ahead and be what we were made to be, without enviously or pride-fully comparing with each other, or trying to be something we aren't (Romans 12:4-5, TM).

∞ What are your thoughts on Romans 12:4-5?

6. **Read Romans 12:6-8.**

∞ Is there something you really like doing, something that comes naturally to you? Describe it.

What you just described is probably one of your gifts. Sometimes it takes effort to uncover and recognize our gifts. But, much of the time they are right in front of you. Quit trying to fit a round peg in a square hole. Stop trying to be anyone else. That is not God's way, and it leads to competition, envy, jealousy, etc. And that is the opposite of living the lifestyle of love.

> *Lifestyle change 5: Accept yourself and accept others as part of God's plan.*

Recognize that God has a purpose for each person, have confidence in that part of His plan.

7. **Read Romans 12:9-10.**

∞ According to these verses, what must love be?

∞ What are you to hate?

∞ To what are you to cling?

> *Lifestyle change 6: Use your gifts and do not compare yourself with other women.*

∞ To whom are you to be devoted?

∞ Whom are you to honor and how?

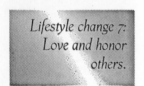

Sincere: genuine, true, not deceitful or hypocritical.

Now isn't this interesting—we are to honor others above ourselves. This is in direct opposition to what the world we live in says. This goes with step 4 of living in humility.

Remember that you are not in control of how another accepts or rejects your love. Quite frankly, you might do nice things for some people who flatly ignore you and all that you do, due to the anger in their own hearts and lives. They may be jealous of you or threatened by you; therefore, they can not honor you or be kind back to you. Just relax,

Lifestyle change 7: Love and honor others.

give every relationship over to God. It is not the end of the world if someone doesn't like you or accept you. Unfair, maybe . . . but not the end of the world. You are responsible for your actions not the actions of others.

8. Read Romans 12: 11-13.

∞ What do you see here that you are to do?

∞ How do you think you can keep your spiritual fervor?

I strongly urge you to memorize Scripture. Nothing will change your life more radically than putting the truth of God's Word in your mind. Stay with one theme or verse for more than a day. Soak it up, let it do its perfect work in you.

I can remember a time when I had lost all desire for anything spiritual. I had been completely let down by ministry and by Christians. My focus was all about *me* and who had let me down. I needed to redirect my focus. I got out the 3 x 5 cards, and I put on a sports watch. Every time that watch beeped, each thirty minutes, I would read a Scripture, from a selected few verses, that I needed at the time. Before long I began to realize that people are just people like me, and people will always let me down. That is life. Christians are no exception. (That is a hard one because we expect perfection out of Christians, don't we? How unfair!) My heart began to soften at the touch of God's Word, and once again my zeal for Jesus began to take root and come alive. And, again I could be:

joyful in hope,
patient in affliction,
faithful in prayer.

And, with the attention and focus off me, I could once again share with God's people and be hospitable in heart and action.

> *Lifestyle change 8: Be joyful and put your hope in God.*

9. Read Romans 12:14. Write this one out!

Whoa! This is the hardest lifestyle change yet. I call this the torture verse because it is torture to my flesh to obey this one. Yet when I do obey this verse, my oh my, do I ever get filled with the peace of God.

These aren't mere words for me, as I have had a few people in my life who have been life's most difficult challenge. Nothing I can do is right with them. I beat myself up for several years, trying to do it my way. Then one day I decided to turn these people over to God completely, and He took the burden. Now, I make it a practice to pray daily for these. I was in the habit of stooping right where they were—arguing, defending, being filled with anger. But, by the grace of God, I now see He has a better way. Bless them!

> *Lifestyle change 9: Bless those who wrong you. Do not stoop to cursing them.*

10. Read Romans 12:15-16.
∞ There are a lot of things here that are significant in a lifestyle change. Make a list of them.

Now begin to use this list as your prayer list.

Lifestyle change 10: Live in harmony with one another.

Again, you can only do your part. But, your part can be huge in being able to stay connected to God, at peace in your heart, and in giving you the ability to look in the mirror each morning. If someone doesn't want harmony, let it go. Just don't make things worse by not taking the directives in Scripture seriously. Anger is usually the thing that gets us in trouble, but God has directions even for that.

In your anger do not sin: when you are on your beds, search your hearts and be silent. Offer right sacrifices and trust in the Lord (Psalm 4:4–5).

This verse has been a great one for me. It is telling me to take a time out when I am angry. Instead of arguing and getting heated up, I am to be silent. Silent? Yes, silent before the Lord, offering a right sacrifice to Him, which is a heart toward God. When I silence everything within me, something wonderful happens to my heart. In a sane place, God can begin leading and directing me in how to handle the person or problem that has made me so angry.

I am not saying deny the anger, but to do as Scripture says: take it to God. I cannot tell you how this one verse has changed my life! Really!

11. Read Romans 12:17-20.

∞ Again, write out these directives in a list.

∞ What are your thoughts about all these things that we are clearly being told should be part of our lifestyle?

12. Write out Romans 12:21. Memorize this one!

Anytime there is a bad thing happening in your life, don't let it over-come you but go to God and let Him transform your life and attitude through the circumstance. If you have a lemon of an experience, then add sugar and make some drinkable lemonade out of it. It could be that God is using the sour to make your life sweeter!

According to Philippians 4:4-8 there is a pattern for adding the sugar of the Spirit to a bad relationship or circumstance:

rejoice in the Lord,

do not be anxious,

pray,

thank God that He is in control,

receive His peace,

think about the good, dwell there,

receive some more of His peace.

13. Can you see how God's Word can be completely functional and prac-tical when we break it down to digest it into our lives?

Now let's review all ten steps of living the lifestyle of love.

1: Offer your life to God completely.

2: Turn away from the world's philosophies.

3: Be changed by filling your mind with God's way.

4: Humble yourself before God.

5: Accept yourself and accept others as part of God's plan.

6: Use your gifts and do not compare yourself with other women.

7: Love and honor others.

8: Be joyful and put your hope in God.

9: Bless those who wrong you. Do not stoop to cursing them.

10: Live in harmony with one another.

Love is a Mighty Fire

Love . . . burns like blazing fire, like a mighty flame. Many waters
cannot quench love; rivers cannot wash it away.
(Song of Songs 8:6-7)

Father,

Living in a new lifestyle requires change, and often I don't have the strength or desire to change. I see clearly from a study in Your Word that I am to live a lifestyle of love, thus changing my normal way of relating to others. I desire to live to please You and want to walk in Your Spirit. Thank You for Your Word and Your instruction on such practical, everyday things. I give my heart to You, work in me. Amen.

ENDNOTES

Introduction
1 Joanne Wallace and Deanna Wallace, "Daily Prayer," *Refreshing as Snow in the Hot Summertime* (Lincoln City, Oregon: Joanne Wallace Publisher, 1998), 68.

One: Living His Love . . . The Key to Life
1 Edward W. Goodrick and John R. Kohlenberger III, *NIV Exhaustive Concordance* (Grand Rapids: Zondervan, 1990), 800-831.
2 Max Lucado, *Just Like Jesus* (Nashville: Word Publishing, 1998), 59.
3 Ibid., 66.

Two: Living Love . . . In Our Daily Choices
1 Lucado, *Just Like Jesus,* 13-14.

Three: Living Love . . . As God Has Loved Us
1 *Roget's II The New Thesaurus,* (Boston: Houghton Mifflin Company, 1980).
2 Chuck Smith, *Living Water* (Eugene, Oregon: Harvest House, 1996), 13.
3 Ibid., 83.
4 Ibid., 85.

Five: Living Love . . . Despite Our Hurts
1 Oswald Chambers, *Conformed to His Image* (Burlington, Ontario: Welch Publishing, 1985), 90.
2 Floyd McClung, Jr. (Seattle: YWAM Publishing, 1992), 28.
3 Henry Gariepy, *Portraits of Christ,* (Grand Rapids: Revell, 1974), quoted by Kirkie Morrissey, *In His Name* (Colorado Springs: NavPress, 1984), 83.

Six: Living Forgiveness . . . True Freedom

1 Karen Burton Mains, *The Key to an Open Heart* (Elgin, Illinois: David Cook Publishing, 1979), 20.

2 Steve Bearden, as quoted by Joanne Wallace, *Starting Over Again,* (Nashville: Thomas Nelson Publishers, 1991), 75.

3 Dr. Henry Cloud and Dr. John Townsend, *12 Christian Beliefs That Can Drive You Crazy* (Grand Rapids: Zondervan, 1995), 75.

Eight: Living Kindness . . . The Refreshed Life

1 Lucado, *Just Like Jesus,* 67.

Nine: Living Real . . . The Practical Side of Love

1 Ruth Harm Calkins, *Lord, Could You Hurry a Little?* (Wheaton: Tyndale House Publishers, 1983), 79.